The Treasure Seeker's Treasury

The
Treasure Seeker's
Treasury

Roy Norvill

HUTCHINSON OF LONDON

Hutchinson & Co (Publishers) Ltd
3 Fitzroy Square, London WIP 6JD

London Melbourne Sydney Auckland
Wellington Johannesburg and agencies
throughout the world

First published 1978
© Roy Norvill 1978

Set in Monotype Imprint
Printed in Great Britain by the Anchor Press Ltd
and bound by Wm Brendon and Son Ltd
both of Tiptree, Essex

ISBN 0 09 131330 9

To Pat – my treasure

Contents

Introduction

Buried treasure has always been a source of eternal speculation and consuming interest. Perhaps it is because everybody enjoys making money and because, in the minds of many, there is a feeling that hidden caches are the easiest way to instant riches. Occasionally this may be so, but usually the trail to a hoard requires intellectual and physical endurance. All too often treasure seekers set off without having done sufficient planning, preparation or research. These form the backbone of treasure seeking, but they must be combined with determination and unwavering belief. Only then can the treasure hunter hope to near his goal.

Belief, however, must never become gullibility. The ability to sort out the tiny grains of truth, sifted in painstaking research from the mountains of rumour which surround all tales of buried riches, is an important attribute. As many treasures are found by researching in libraries and museums as by digging in the field with pick and shovel.

In this book I have recounted the classic stories of landlocked treasure. They are the classics because of the fabulous wealth involved. Some have been partially discovered by amateurs, and this adds further evidence of their authenticity. There is however a word of caution that is best passed on by recounting a story told by the late and renowned Colonel Fawcett. He recalled hiding £60 of gold that he had previously found when his baggage become overweight on one South American exploration. When he passed by later he was told that an Englishman had come that way and had buried £60000 of treasure some years before. Of course the glowing accounts made no mention of the fact that he had retrieved the cache later. 'Let would-be treasure hunters ponder the moral of this tale,' he said, and well we ought.

But despite Colonel Fawcett's caution, the treasure seeker should never let his imagination be stifled. Hunting may at times be a soul-destroying business: detractors will often point to the Oak Island Money Pit as proof of the fact that ardent treasure seekers have to spend a fortune and often finish up without any reward. Yet there must be a reason for the over-whelming evidence of treasure on Oak Island and today we have a multitude of technological advantages for finding it. Long and arduous travel is comparatively cheap and easy, equipment is available to buy or hire, and photography, the telephone and the radio allow the determined hunter to check his facts in the field. In short, the treasure seeker of today risks far less than his predecessors and so has a much greater chance of discovering hidden riches. Luck still plays her part, but so she does in any rewarding endeavour, and diligent research is still the key to successful hunting.

To the sceptic I would point out the rewards other than money that are there for the taking. Should you find yourself suffering at a desk from any of the commercial sicknesses like nerves, ulcers or simply boredom, you will find that a mild treasure hunt is the greatest therapy in the world – mainly because your objective is never in doubt. The treasure is there and once you have found it your worries will be over.

I am not going to claim that treasure seeking is always a quick way to riches. Legal wrangles can begin as you try to sell your find. I remember meeting the American marine archaeologist and treasure hunter, Robert Marx, in 1970 when he was living in Grand Bahama Island. He was just back from investigating the sites of the lost Mayan cities in Guatemala. Bob and I went diving over an old Spanish wreck off the Lucayan Beach where a large collection of Spanish silver coins had been discovered some eighteen months previously. I was told that the lucky finders had become involved in a legal case and would be fortunate if ownership of the haul was eventually settled on them. At that time the coins were in a bank vault in Freeport, and when I left in September 1971 they had only just been released for sale.

So if you know a little about the law, have a working knowledge of geology, history and archaeology combined with the rudiments of map-reading, cryptology languages and perhaps a smattering of mining engineering, you are ready for the treasure hunt. Diving is for experts, and so in the following chapters I have confined myself to the landlocked treasures which can still be unearthed by eager and informed amateurs. There is no doubt in my mind that there is still plenty there for the taking and, while I would not advise an overseas expedition for your first hunt, the following stories supply the groundwork of facts on which the enthusiast can base his detailed research. From there the determined treasure hunter can leave his arm-chair and set out for the well-deserved riches that are surely his.

The Treasures of Cocos Island

Of all stories of hidden treasure, the sagas of Cocos Island must surely be the best known. Many are the novels that owe their drama and inspiration to the extraordinary events which took place on that remote little hump of land – probably the most famous is Robert Louis Stevenson's *Treasure Island*. Yet Cocos Island (not to be confused with the group of islands of the same name, also called the Keeling Islands) is far from being the romantic and tropical paradise that is portrayed by novelists. It is situated at 5 degrees 32 minutes latitude North, 87 degrees 10 minutes longitude West, a bearing which places it some 300 miles south-west of the Republic of Costa Rica, to which country the island belongs.

The abundance of cocoa trees gave the island its name. It is about four miles long and six wide, most of the coastline consisting of sheer, rocky cliff, especially on the eastern side, where the escarpments vary in height from 200 to 600 feet. Inland is a rocky plateau covered with tropical vegetation and in most places the undergrowth is so dense that explorers have to follow the rocky beds of streams to escape the strenuous task of cutting their way through brush. The trees are dense and their entwined branches, laced with heavy moss, cast a perpetual darkness on the ground below. Huge boulders and precipitous hills stand on all sides. Vast clouds of insects plague all visitors.

Three volcanic peaks dominate the island: the highest, Mount Iglesia (Grand Summit), is 2788 feet. The others are about 1500 feet and are not officially named: one is known as

West Summit and the other is called South Cone, or Mount Runder.

Two main bays are accessible to shipping, both having fresh water springs and both being in the north of the island. One is Chatham Bay; the other Wafer Bay. There is a third small inlet where a landing could easily be made, a place called the Bay of Hope in the south. Here two small streams flow, one into the bay and the other to the sea some three-quarters of a mile to the east. When it rains heavily, a waterfall forms as the rain cascades off the nearby hills and pours into the sea.

During the winter it rains steadily for days at a time, and heavy mists hang thick over the jungle. In the summer it steams with tropical heat and the temperature frequently stands at $115°F$, with the humidity so oppressive that Europeans can endure the labour of digging for only a few hours at a time.

The great legend of Cocos Island's treasure begins towards the end of the pirate era in the West Indies between the years 1683 and 1700. The freebooters had been forced out of their stronghold in Tortuga and had re-established themselves in Jamaica's Port Royal. But this was not to last, for in 1692 the town was devastated by an earthquake and it sank into the sea. The pirates scattered, some to Nassau and some into the Indian Ocean.

The Pacific, however, still had rich pickings for the enterprising sea rover and one such was an Englishman, Captain Edward Davis, who raided the coast of New Spain from Baja California down to Guayaquil in his ship, *Bachelor's Delight*. He used Cocos Island as a headquarters and it is thought that he buried several chests of treasure somewhere on the island before he gave up pirating, in answer to the amnesty offered by King James II, and settled on the Virginia coast. Retirement, however, did not apparently suit the adventurous Captain Davis, for in 1702 he acquired a small vessel and returned to Cocos Island to take up pirating once more. After an unsuccessful attack on the town of Porto Bello, he disappeared completely and his end has remained a mystery.

Over a hundred years later, in 1819, a pirate called Benito Bonito, or 'Bonito of the Bloody Sword' – thought by some to be an English naval officer named Bennet Graham – came ashore at a spot near Acapulco, Mexico, and seized a rich cargo of gold, which he took to Cocos Island and buried in the sandstone shore of Wafer Bay. He then announced that he was sailing for the West Indies, a plan disagreeable to part of the crew, who mutinied. Bonito lived up to his nickname and ruthlessly quelled the rising. Bones of men found years later were believed to be the remains of these sailors. Bonito and his Bloody Sword sailed away to the West Indies where in 1821 he was killed in a battle with a British man o' war, so never returning to claim his buried loot.

At about this time, the armies of Simon Bolivar were gradually overthrowing the Spanish regime in South America. In 1823, as the revolutionary army approached Lima, civil and religious authorities made hurried plans for both their escape and the salvage of their accumulated riches. Some buried their treasure, and others sent theirs up the coast on pack animals to the new republics. One especially valuable collection was that of the great cathedral of Lima: gold and silver artifacts, most encrusted with jewels, including not only gold statues and candlesticks, but also an image of the Virgin Mary holding the Divine Child which was reputed to be made of solid gold and liberally garnished with precious stones.

As the army approached, this wealth was taken to the sea port of Callao only eight miles from Lima, but to the refugees' horror there were no Spanish vessels available. The most likely ship in the harbour was the *Mary Dear* (or *Mary Dier*) under the command of a Scottish captain, William Thompson. The treasure was therefore loaded aboard together with six soldiers and two priests to guard it and Thompson was commissioned to cruise off the coast of Peru for several weeks. If Lima was not captured, he was to return to Callao and hand back the cargo; otherwise he was to deliver it to the Spanish authorities in Panama.

After some time at sea, the thought of the immense fortune lying below decks proved too much for Thompson and his crew. The guards were murdered and thrown overboard and the *Mary Dear* sailed for Cocos Island.

Thompson anchored in Chatham Bay, and then took eleven longboat loads of treasure ashore and hid it in a cave. Several chests of gold were shared out among the crew and they then set sail. Shortly after leaving the island, however, they were sighted by the Spanish frigate *Espeigle* which engaged and captured them. When the Spaniards discovered the remains of the Lima treasure, as it had come to be known, they hanged all the members of the crew except Thompson and his First Mate, who were spared on condition that they disclosed the secret of the hiding place.

Returning to Cocos Island, Thompson and the Mate went ashore with a large party of the Spaniards and led them into the densest part of the undergrowth. Then they took their opportunity and, tricking the guards, fled into the jungle. After a week of fruitless searching the Spaniards gave up and sailed away.

Several months later, a whaling ship called in at Chatham Bay to replenish her water supplies. Crew members found the two men ill and half starved on the beach. They were taken to Puntarenas, Costa Rica, but the Mate died of fever about a week after and only Thompson survived to remain with the whaler until she reached her home port in Newfoundland.

From this point on, the Cocos Island story becomes a tangle of conflicting claims, facts and fiction, but the account which follows is accepted by most historians and gains support from existing documents and records.

Thompson continued his life as a seaman, but was apparently never able to get enough money to organize for a ship to return and recover the treasure. While on a transatlantic voyage, he became firm friends with another sailor by the name of John Keating. By 1841 Thompson was in poor health and realized that his chances of getting back to Cocos Island were slim, so he shared the secret of the buried hoard with Keating.

Thompson returned to Newfoundland and died in 1844. On his deathbed, he gave Keating a map showing the exact location of the treasure and a letter of instructions for finding the cache. One story is that it was placed in a natural cave below the ground, with the entrance concealed by a large boulder so balanced on the cave rim that it could be turned aside by placing an iron bar into a hole the size of a man's thumb and applying pressure.

Keating succeeded in finding a wealthy shipowner who agreed to finance the voyage on the condition that his own captain, Captain Boag (or Bogue), be placed in command of the vessel, something to which Keating could only agree. By the time Keating and Boag arrived at Cocos Island, the crew had discovered the reason for their voyage and were contemplating mutiny once the treasure had been located.

Anchoring in Chatham Bay, Keating and Boag went ashore alone. With the aid of the directions and the map, they located the cache with very little difficulty. Confronted by the sight of the vast hoard, they decided to keep it from the rest of the crew, and take only as much as they could comfortably carry in their pockets. Then they closed the treasure cave and returned to the ship, telling their shipmates that they had been unable to find it. The two men intended to sell what they had found and buy another boat with the proceeds so that they could return later.

But their demeanour must have given them away. They were disbelieved and threatened until they agreed to take the crew to the cave the following morning. That night under cover of darkness, Keating and Boag slipped over the side and swam to the island to hide in the dense jungle. For several days the frustrated crew searched without success. Finally they gave up and sailed away.

No one really knows what happened next, but when – months later – a ship called in for water, the crew found only Keating alive. There seems to be little doubt that Keating returned home with at least a small part of the treasure, but estimates of the quantity vary considerably: it was probably only a small portion. Nevertheless, on his return to Newfoundland, Keating purchased business property in St John's and a large farm near the city. An attempt was made to charge him with the murder of Boag, but Keating maintained that he was accidentally drowned and, in the absence of any evidence, the indictment came to nothing. Later evidence, although flimsy, seems to indicate that he killed Boag and buried him in the treasure cave. It is also extremely likely that he removed some of the treasure to another hiding place, probably to the Bay of Hope in the south of the island.

In the early 1870s Keating had become a sick and destitute old man. One of his few friends at the time was another roving sailor, Nicholas Fitzgerald, and Keating disclosed the secret to him, in an attempt to persuade Fitzgerald to organize an expedition to recover the treasure. Fitzgerald's doubts about the enterprise were reinforced when Keating insisted on making one stipulation, namely that he was not asked to go into the cave.

'The agreement was not carried out,' Fitzgerald wrote later. 'Believing that Captain Boag . . . had mysteriously disappeared while in his company on Cocos Island, I thought I would be running a grave risk of my life to go single-handed with him. The disappearance of Boag was unsatisfactorily explained to me by him.' Nicholas Fitzgerald appears to have been an itinerant character and was probably in any case never wealthy enough to afford to fit out a ship for the expedition.

Before he died, however, Keating passed on the map and letter which he had inherited from Thompson – along with another letter giving the location of a cache in the Bay of Hope. This may have been part of the original cache that Keating himself had moved, but there is no definite evidence. The first letter stated:

Turn your back on the sea and then make your way towards the mountain that is in the north of the island. On the mountain slope you will see a brook to the west. Cross this and go twenty more paces due west. Then take fifty paces towards the centre of the island until the sea is completely hidden behind the mountain. At the place where the ground suddenly falls away you will see a white mark on the rock. That is where the cave is. It has a well hidden entrance covered by a stone slab and the tunnel entrance leads sideways into a chamber.

This letter, of course, relates to the landing place at Chatham Bay. The second letter gives another set of instructions:

Disembark in the Bay of Hope between two islets in water five fathoms deep. Walk 350 paces along the course of the stream then turn NNE for 850 yards – stake – setting sun – stake – draws silhouette of an eagle with wings spread. At the extremity of sun and shadow; cave marked with a cross. Here lies the treasure.

Later explorers have remarked on the fact that when the setting sun is in perigee with Grand Summit (Mount Iglesia), it projects a shadow that resembles an eagle's head. In winter the sun sets in the north-west, projecting the shadow into the Bay of Hope.

At one time in his wandering career, Fitzgerald is said to have made an inventory of the Lima treasure. Whether his inventory was copied from one compiled by Keating is not known, but the document was left in Coiba and found some time later in a museum in Caracas. Later still, it was said to have come into the possession of one of Fitzgerald's closest friends, Commodore Curzon-Howe and it is known that Howe and Fitzgerald exchanged correspondence prior to the latter's death, in which Fitzgerald revealed all that he knew about the treasure cache. Howe himself made no attempt to go to Cocos but merely passed the documents on to his son. The inventory (whose authenticity has not been established beyond doubt) reads:

We have buried at a depth of four feet in the red earth:
- 1 chest: Altar trimmings of cloth and gold, with baldachins monstrances, chalices, comprising 1244 stones.
- 1 chest: 2 gold reliquaries weighing 120 pounds, with 624 topazes, cornelians and emeralds, 12 diamonds.
- 1 chest: 3 reliquaries of cast metal weighing 160 pounds with 860 rubies and various stones. 19 diamonds.
- 1 chest: 4000 doubloons of Spain marked '8', 5000 crowns of Mexico, 124 swords, 64 dirks, 120 shoulder belts, 28 rondaches.
- 1 chest: 8 caskets of cedarwood and silver with 3840 cut stones, rings, patens and 4265 uncut stones.

28 feet to the north-east at a depth of eight feet in the yellow sand:
7 chests with 22 candelabras in gold and silver weighing 250 pounds, and 164 rubies a foot.

12 armspans west at a depth of ten feet in the red earth:
A seven-foot Virgin of gold, with the child Jesus, and her crown and pectoral of 780 pounds rolled in her gold chasuble on which there are 4-inch emeralds on the pectoral and six are 6-inch topazes on the crown, the seven crosses are of diamonds.

The story of the cache became so well known that Cocos Island was visited by a steady stream of treasure seekers. Early in the year 1872, Captain Thomas Welsh sailed his brig *Laura* into Chatham Bay under the title of the South Pacific Hidden Treasure Company. Welsh believed that he had exact information for locating the Lima treasure, but though the company dug a tunnel some 200 feet into the mountain – an exercise which occupied them for five gruelling months – they found nothing. Keating's widow, who possessed a map, also organized an expedition, but it returned to Newfoundland without ever getting as far as Cocos Island.

In 1875 a boat owned by the Pacific Steam Navigation Company anchored off the island. One of the crew members, Bob Flower, was struggling through the undergrowth in search of the cache when he slipped and fell down a sharp incline into a hollow. Here he spotted some gold coins. He put some in his pocket and scrambled out with difficulty, then made his way back to the main party. Afterwards, he was unable to retrace his exact steps to the site of the hollow.

But this was not the last of the discoveries on Cocos Island. One of the most interesting stories is that of a German sailor, August Gissler, who in 1880 was serving aboard a ship carrying Portuguese labourers and immigrants from the Azores to Hawaii. One of the passengers became firm friends with Gissler and before the voyage ended confided to him that he was the owner of a treasure chart bequeathed to him by his grandfather. The old parchment indicated that treasure had been buried on an island named 'Las Palmas'. Gissler further learned that the passenger's grandfather had once sailed with Benito Bonito. Although somewhat sceptical, Gissler made a rough copy of the chart and kept it for future reference. Eight years later he settled in Hawaii, where through a family marriage he became related to a white man known as 'Old Mac'. Somehow he discovered that Old Mac himself possessed a treasure map, and after much coercion Gissler finally persuaded him to compare it with his own. They reached the conclusion that the island depicted in Gissler's map could only be Cocos

Island, and at last Gissler became interested enough to take an active part in the hunting for the treasure. He set off for Cocos Island and there spent several months in an utterly fruitless search. Frustrated, he went to Costa Rica and took up residence there.

But he had not abandoned hope. In 1894 Gissler returned to the treasure island and settled there, this time with full legal rights inasmuch as he had been made the first Governor of the island by the Costa Rican authorities. He settled in the north-east corner at Wafer Bay and established a plantation so that he could live while he searched for the treasure. In the same year, Keating's widow arrived to make a search. Keating had told her about a great stone with a 'K' carved in it and an arrow pointing to a hollow tree. Gissler found the spot, almost obscured by dense foliage. There was a rusty iron cable attached to a hook, long enough for a man to reach the bottom of the tree, but no sign of the treasure.

It is said that Keating's widow eventually remarried a man named Brennan. On Brennan's death, she gave the map to a Captain Thomas Hackett, who in turn passed it on to Fred M. Hackett of Victoria, British Columbia. From here, it went to a Captain Gus Whidden and then, it is said, to Gissler. There may well be a discrepancy in this story, for it seems surprising that Gissler was lucky enough to come into possession of two maps, the first of Bonito's hidden cache and the second of the Lima treasure. If he did obtain the Lima treasure map it must have been well towards the end of his long stay on the island.

In 1897 two English cruisers, the *Champion* and the *Impericus*, under Admiral Henry Palliser dropped anchor in Wafer Bay at a time when Gissler was visiting the Costa Rican mainland. Three hundred sailors went ashore, and in two or three days, turned Gissler's private estate into a wilderness with spades and dynamite. Palliser found nothing and the Costa Ricans made a formal protest to the British government. Five years later, when the Admiral had retired, he returned as a private citizen to land at Chatham Bay, having somehow acquired information that had once belonged to Fitzgerald. It did him no good. Again he found nothing.

In 1903 a man named Christian Cruse arrived on the island,

having acquired the rights as 'Island Governor' from a free and easy Costa Rican government who had overlooked the fact that they had already made Gissler the Governor. Cruse had become friendly with one of England's richest peers, Lord Fitzwilliam, who arrived in his yacht *Veronica* and put his hundred-man crew to work to try and unearth the treasure. When Lord Fitzwilliam was accidentally hit on the head by a piece of rock during dynamiting in Chatham Bay work came to a halt, and the search was called off.

Gissler himself had died almost penniless in a New York rooming house in 1930. He had lived on the island for more than twenty years and during that time had found only old camp sites, rusty arms, pots, rum bottles, skeletons and a Spanish doubloon dated 1788.

In the years that followed Fitzwilliam's abortive expedition many more such attempts were made, some by world-famous personalities. One was the well-known racing driver, Sir Malcolm Campbell. Before he set out on his expedition, Campbell consulted a spiritualist and in the seance that took place he was told that 'the treasure lies high up, perhaps a thousand feet above sea level'. In February 1926 Sir Malcolm arrived in his yacht *Adventurer* and anchored in Wafer Bay. He had detailed information about the history of the island and hoped not only to locate the treasure, but to clear up the mystery of Boag's death as well. In the book* he subsequently wrote on his experiences he recorded a notable, if inconclusive incident. He and his mongrel dog were trying to sleep one night in the tropical heat.

Suddenly, the dog who had been sleeping beside me, leapt to his feet with a terrifying howl and dashed to the open flap of the tent, barking with rage and fear. He was almost beside himself. I have never seen a dog in such a paroxysm of terror. It was as though he had seen a ghost. He stood there barking and yapping into the blackness of the night, every hair on end, his voice vibrant with fear and defiance. I took my revolver from the holster and crawled to the tent door, expecting to meet anything from a ghost to a wild pig or

---

*Details of this, and other books I mention in the text, will be found in the List of Further Reading on page 173.

an Indian on his belly. There was nothing. The great wood fire, built to keep off the insects, leapt and flickered redly against the background of the tropic dark. Overhead, a million stars shone and twinkled like points of fire. . . .

I stepped quietly outside the radius of the firelight and snaked among the trees. . . . I could find nothing, although I scouted cautiously round all the camp. All the time the dog was standing in the tent doorway, whining and shivering. I had the feeling that, somewhere in the blackness, someone was watching me, following my every movement. I returned to the tent with a prickly feeling down my spine.

Twice after this, the same thing happened in the middle of the night. We could not account for it and I cannot explain it now. There are no animals on the island so far as I know, except wild pigs and they are not stealthy beasts. . . . They plunge and crash and do not care who listens to them. I saw no rats, no snakes, in fact no reptiles or mammals of any sort apart from a pig. What then, or who, could have been our mysterious midnight visitor?

Sir Malcolm and his companions were not fortunate in their search for the treasure, but just how close they were to success was revealed some six years later.

The first small hint came in 1931, when a Belgian named Bergmans found a two-foot-long Madonna of gold in the Bay of Hope. He was able to sell it for about 11 000 dollars. A year later a certain Colonel Leckie and an electrical engineer named Clayton visited Wafer Bay with the 'Metallophon', a newly invented metal detector. Twelve yards from where Sir Malcolm Campbell had sunk his shaft, they located the hoard of Benito Bonito.

Spurred on by the success of the Leckie expedition, a constant stream of treasure hunters continued to visit the island, large sums of money being invested in the gamble. £70 000 was spent by the London Treasure Recovery Company in fitting out the *Queen of Scots* in 1933, and in October 1934 she arrived at Cocos Island. There is no record that any of the party ever found anything. Captain Max Stanton of Melbourne went there after serving as chief officer of the *Discovery* in Moreton's Antarctic Expedition of 1930–1. He later said that 'ghosts of dead men interfered' with his search and caused him to abandon it. A Captain Bellamy (or Ballamy) claimed to have found 133 gold and silver coins in the sand, but malaria forced him to give up the search.

In 1937 the 'Sea Devil', Count Luckner, arrived to make a search based on his possession of an old map, but the treasure evaded him also. Another unlucky party was the American Forbes Expedition of early 1940, who took to Cocos Island all kinds of technical equipment and information passed on by a relation of Forbes who claimed to possess letters left by Thompson. They believed the treasure to be hidden under two feet of stone and pebbles and covered by a rag mattress and they did find the remains of a cedarwood coffer that had once been wrapped in chamois leather. According to the accounts, part of the treasure had been stored in that manner. They also found one of the landmarks in the documents. In following years, they mounted four more similar expeditions and in 1948 found in the sand near the creek which flows into Chatham Bay a length of exquisitely formed gold chain and a piece of petrified sailcloth. As a result of this, Forbes now believes that, owing to geological changes over the years, the cache lies under water at high tide, near the mouth of the creek.

In 1953 a London firm, Ocean Enterprise Ltd, searched but found nothing. In 1955 a converted submarine chaser, the *Isle of Capri* with fourteen men, came to Cocos Island. Their leader, Charles Williams, had with him a 130-year-old map and part of the cargo consisted of electronic detectors, two bull-dozers, compressed-air drills and hydraulic pumps, as well as electric winches. They found nothing.

In recent years the Costa Rican government has had to be considered a great deal more than on previous occasions. In the case of the *Isle of Capri* expedition, they demanded 50 per cent of any profits resulting from the treasure hunt. From the first Forbes expedition they had only demanded a quarter, but lately, they have been declining permission of any kind if the expedition's object is treasure. Dr Hans Hass, the underwater explorer, was given permission to dive off the Cocos Island coast only on condition that he was not searching for the treasure.

Is there, in fact, any treasure left on the island? Captain Edward Davis' cache is undocumented and although it is not impossible that he really did conceal treasure there, it is best discounted as legend. Benito Bonito's hoard was both authentic and discovered. This leaves the Lima treasure, the largest of the three caches. Of that the larger part may indeed be still hidden.

Cocos Island, of course, has not escaped the geological changes of the last 150 years and the landscape may have been considerably affected. A quantity of evidence points to the Bay of Hope as being the likely spot for part of the cache to be hidden. Explorer Tony Mangel, who thought that the treasure might be found within 'a 100 yards of 5 degrees 30' 17" North – 87 degrees 0' 40" West', found a cave in the bay which was accessible for about an hour every low tide. The Belgian in 1931 who discovered the gold Madonna, did so because he acted on this information.

As I have stated, I believe that this is because Keating moved part of the treasure after Boag's demise. Referring to the inventory given to Fitzgerald by Keating, it is worth noting that the red earth and the yellow sand together, mentioned in the document, can be found at the Bay of Hope.

Connelly's Lost Emeralds

Stewart Connelly, an American, was born on 9 December 1899, and in the last few months of the First World War joined the armed forces and served on active duty. Like many he had no ties when he was discharged and so he spent several years wandering until finally he settled in Madrid. There he spent much of this time in the Biblioteca Nacional studying the Spanish conquest of South America, a subject in which he became deeply interested. In the course of his reading he chanced upon a small volume written by a monk, Sanchez, who had accompanied Pizarro on his expedition. One section of this book indicated that the *conquistadores* had learned of the existence of emerald fields situated somewhere in the remote interior of what is now Ecuador.

There were enough clues to the location to arouse Connelly's interest, and he made up his mind to search for the emeralds. Leaving Madrid, he worked his way to Quito where he studied all the available maps of the surrounding jungle. Sometime in 1924 he finally set out, alone, following the river eastwards until he reached the Rio Napo, nine or ten days' journey from Quito. This was to be his starting point.

In the archives of the Director of Mines in Quito lie his account of his expedition, now partly destroyed, and there he relates how he had learned that it was not only impractical but in all known instances fatal for a white man to enter the forbidden territory of certain savage Indian tribes – the territory where, according to Sanchez, the lost emerald mine of the Incas was to be found. Connelly, however, had devised what he considered to be a foolproof scheme to protect himself against the hostility of these tribes. In his words:

I therefore decided to enter the jungle in such a manner as to make the Indians believe I was demented. For some strange reason, jungle savages have in the past befriended and at times revered crazy men, and I hoped that the little bamboo flute that I carried would serve to set me apart from normal people. No sooner had I crossed the Rio Napo and entered the deep jungle than I began blowing the flute, sending crazy staccato notes through the stillness of the green wilderness. I blindly followed a dozen or more trails but, using my compass, always walked in a north-easterly direction.

Connelly estimated that he averaged about two miles an hour for nine days. Then he was discovered by a tribe of wild Indians known as the Corinahuas. He acted the role of madman well enough to convince the savages, for they took him in. With them he lived for the next three months, learning their ways and how they survived in the jungle.

Leaving this tribe, he continued alone through the jungle, steadily moving to the north-east and, after five days, he came to the banks of a river. Here he encountered a tribe much more savage than the Corinahuas. Again his antics with the flute saved him and, after a battle of wits with the tribe's witch-doctor, they allowed him to stay with them.

Life with this primitive, savage tribe drove me nearly to the brink of insanity. I had to keep up my masquerade as the wielder of supernatural powers and could never forget for a moment that I had to live and act as one demented. As the crow flies, it was my impression that I was about one hundred air miles from Puerto Napo, the small village on the banks of the Napo river that had been my starting point. By following trails, however, I gauged the distance to be exceedingly more and guessed that I had covered probably two or three hundred land miles. The village of the Orijones lay on a bend in the river which they called the *Numba*, meaning in their dialect 'river of blood'. The terrain in the immediate vicinity was hilly and farther to the east were huge, black cliffs, while in the distance lay a series of irregularly-shaped, snow-capped peaks.

After he had been several months with the tribe, their natural suspicion of him began to relax and he was taken along on hunting trips. On one occasion he was allowed to accompany a young warrior of the tribe, whose name was Katuku, in search of game.

For two days we travelled eastward where the best hunting grounds were to be found. On the morning of the third day we came into the black, barren hills and following a rock-strewn valley, suddenly we were confronted by a tremendous precipice of black, crumbly slate flecked with large pieces of white quartz. We stopped at the foot of the cliff and saw, scattered among the white stones, dozens of emeralds. I knew I had rediscovered the lost emerald mine of the Incas, and that with a little luck and the blessings of God, I could reap a green fortune that would stagger the imagination. I hoped desperately that Katuku was not watching as I carelessly, so as not to attract his attention, bent over and picked up a handful of emeralds, none of them smaller than a walnut, and carefully placed them in my shoulder pouch. At this moment, I had but one thought in mind – would I be able to retrace my steps from Puerto Napo to my newly discovered fabulous green treasure, for now that my quest was over, I fully intended to return and reap a just reward, which after months of torture and suffering, I felt I was entitled to.

On his return to the village, Connelly secretly prepared to return to civilization. He well knew that the Indians would not willingly allow him to go, so he bided his time until the tribe held a feast in celebration of good hunting. Elated in the knowledge that his chance to escape was imminent, Connelly allowed himself to drink sparingly of the heady potent brew, that the natives consumed in quantity on such occasions. It was then that Connelly made the mistake that was to prove almost fatal. For a long time Katuku had admired the mad white man's strange shiny bauble – his compass. On this occasion, Katuku once more asked if he could have it. Intoxicated with the thought of the immense fortune within his grasp, Connelly surrendered it.

In the early hours of the morning, taking advantage of the Indians' stupor, Connelly slipped out of the village and into the jungle. He was successful in eluding them but without the aid of the compass he lost his way. For weeks he wandered about, with only the knowledge gained by his life with the natives to help him survive. But survive he did, and he made it back to the Rio Napo. After swimming the river, he collapsed exhausted on the bank. Fortunately, he had come out of the jungle close to the little church outpost of Ahuana and he was found by two of the Spanish missionaries.

Having recovered, he made his way back to Quito and went to the authorities to stake his claim to the emerald mine. But he was unable to make a legal claim because he could not give a satisfactory location. After some discussion, it was arranged that, if he wrote out a detailed statement describing the way he found the mine, the Ecuadorian government would grant him a temporary concession – to be finalized at a later date, when it became possible properly to survey the site.

Connelly had to agree to this and forthwith wrote his account. Then he sold the emeralds that he had brought out with him and prepared to equip an expedition. With a carefully selected crew, he set out from Puerto Napo in 1925 in an effort to retrace his steps. The expedition was never heard of again.

Ten years later the authorities decided that it was safe to assume that Connelly and the members of his expedition had not survived the jungle, and consequently made the account public.

From the information given in the account, it seems likely that the mine lies up near the border of Napo Bastaza Province, Ecuador, and Putumayo Province of Colombia. In fact, the possibility of the site actually being in Colombia is far from remote. Colombia is famed for its emeralds, a green variety of mineral beryl which crystallizes into long, six-sided prisms. In ancient times Egypt was the prime source of the gem, but nowadays the best stones come from either the Urals or Colombia.

As far as is known, the emerald mine has not been rediscovered, but anyone who has sufficient funds to organize an expedition using a helicopter will find certain landmarks in the account helpful. For those who consider going on foot, the territory is still as wild today as it was in 1925. Connelly had a fantastic stroke of luck; it failed to hold.

28.

The Great Tunnels of Peru

One of the most fantastic and seemingly improbable treasure stories appeared in print for the first time in 1887, when Madame H. P. Blavatsky published her two volumes entitled *Isis Unveiled*. There she touches on the attribution of ancient ruins, found on both American continents and many West Indian islands, to the legendary submerged Atlantis, and goes on to say that the magicians, that is the priests, of the now submerged continent had a network of tunnels running in all directions.

Madame Blavatsky travelled extensively throughout South America in 1851 and it was at this time that she was told of a vast tunnel existing under Peru. A few years later what she had thought merely a curious legend was confirmed by an Italian who had tried to verify the story in a most remarkable way. His name is not known but he revealed that he had acquired secret evidence from an old priest, who had received it from a Peruvian Indian at confession. The Italian further explained that he was adept at the art of hypnotism, and that the priest was compelled to make the revelation to him while under his hypnotic influence.

The story is connected with the famous treasure of the Emperor Atahualpa, the last of the Incas, and, according to the Peruvian, it had been well-known to all Indians of the higher class since the great Inca's murder. The tale of the Spaniards' treachery to the Inca Atahualpa is familiar. He was made prisoner by Pizarro, the Spanish leader, and in an attempt to have him released, his Queen offered in exchange for his life a room full of gold 'from the floor to the ceiling, as high up as his conqueror could reach', to be delivered before sunset three days later. She kept her promise, but Pizarro broke his. Filled with greed at the sight of so much treasure, the conqueror declared that he would not release Atahualpa but would murder him, unless the Queen revealed the place from where the treasure came. He had already heard rumours that the Incas possessed a hidden, inexhaustible mine, a subterranean tunnel running for many miles underground, in which were kept the accumulated riches of the country.

The Queen begged for delay, and went to consult the oracles. During the sacrifice, the chief priest showed her, by an ancient means of divination in the consecrated 'black mirror', that the murder of her husband was unavoidable, whether or not she delivered the treasure to Pizarro. At this, the Queen gave the order to close the door that formed the entrance cut in the rocky wall of a chasm. Under the direction of priests and magicians, the chasm was then filled to the top with huge boulders and the surface covered to conceal all traces of the work. Atahualpa was murdered and his Queen committed suicide, while the secret of the tunnels was locked in the breasts of a few faithful Peruvians.

Madame Blavatsky was told that various governments had sent search parties, but they had failed to locate the tunnels. Peruvian historians of the time had corroborated the tradition. Several years after hearing the story, and its corroboration by the Italian, Madame Blavatsky again visited Peru. Going southward from Lima by water, she and her companions reached a point near Arica at sunset, and they were struck by the appearance of an enormous rock, nearly perpendicular, standing solitary on the shore, apart from the ranges of the Andes. It was, she was convinced, the rock known as the Tomb of the Incas. As the last rays of the setting sun struck the face of the rock, she could make out, with an ordinary opera-glass, some curious hieroglyphics inscribed on the volcanic surface.

Madame Blavatsky relates in her book how, as the capital of Peru, Cuzco contained a temple of the sun, famed for its magnificence. It was roofed with thick plates of gold, and the walls were covered with the same precious metal; the gutters

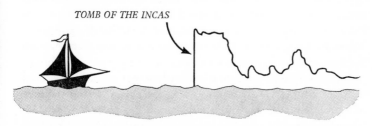

*The hieroglyphics cut in bas-relief in the rock known as the
Tomb of the Incas at Ylo, taken from Madame Blavatsky's map.*

were also of solid gold. In the west wall the architects contrived
an aperture in such a way that when the sunbeams reached it,
it focused them inside the building, illuminating the idols and
disclosing mystic signs at other times invisible. It was only by
understanding these hieroglyphics that the secret of the tunnel
and its approaches could be learned. One such approach,
she said, lay in the neighbourhood of Cuzco.

TOMB OF THE INCAS

*A drawing of the outline of the Tomb of the Incas taken from
the margin of Madame Blavatsky's own map.*

This leads directly into an immense tunnel which runs from Cuzco
to Lima [about 380 miles] and then, turning southward, extends into
Bolivia [now Chile]. At a certain point it is intersected by a royal
tomb. Inside this sepulchral chamber are cunningly arranged two
doors; or, rather, two enormous slabs which turn upon pivots, and
close so tightly as to be only distinguishable from the other portions
of the sculptured walls by the secret signs, whose key is in the
possession of the faithful custodians. One of these turning slabs
covers the southern mouth of the Lima tunnel – the other, the
northern one of the Bolivian corridor. The latter, running southward,
passes through Trapaca and Cobijo, for Arica is not far away from

the little river called Pay'quina, which is the boundary between Peru and Bolivia.

Not far from this spot stand three separate peaks which form a curious triangle; they are included in the chain of the Andes. According to tradition the only practicable entrance to the corridor leading northward is in one of these peaks; but without the secret of its landmarks, a regiment of Titans might rend the rocks in vain in the attempt to find it. But even were someone to gain an entrance and find his way as far as the turning slab in the wall of the sepulchre, and attempt to blast it out, the superincumbent rocks are so disposed as to bury the tomb, its treasures, and – as the mysterious Peruvian expressed it to us – 'a thousand warriors' in one common ruin. There is no other access to the Arica chamber but through the door in the mountain near Pay'quina. Along the entire length of the corridor, from Bolivia to Lima and Cuzco, are smaller hiding places filled with treasures of gold and precious stone, the accumulations of many generations of Incas, the aggregate value of which is incalculable.

Madame Blavatsky claimed to possess an accurate plan of the tunnel, the sepulchre, and the doors, given to her by an old Peruvian. If she had ever thought of profiting by the secret, it would have required the cooperation of the Peruvian and Bolivian governments on an extensive scale. To say nothing of physical obstacles, no one individual or small party could undertake such an exploration without encountering the army of smugglers and brigands with which the coast was infested. There, however, the treasure lies, and there the tradition said it would lie till the last vestige of Spanish rule disappeared from the whole of North and South America. Such is Madame Blavatsky's fabulous tale.

This legend is also included in a book written by the late Harold T. Wilkins, entitled *Mysteries of Ancient South America*. Wilkins gives a plan of the tunnel which he compiled from totally different sources, not having read Madame Blavatsky's account until his book was going to press. Unfortunately, Wilkins' plan seems to owe so much to his imagination I scoffed loud and long at what appeared to be a tall story when I first read it. However, recent explorations in the area make it almost certain that there is more truth than fiction in the story.

Apart from well-known tunnel systems in the rest of the

world – notably India and Turkey – there have been unverified reports of huge, subterranean tunnels in Central and South America before. John L. Stephens in his book *Incidents of Travel in Central America* reported a visit in 1841 to the ruined city of Santa Cruz del Quiche, in Guatemala. In the company of the local padre, who acted as a guide, Stevens made a tour of the ruins.

Under one of the buildings was an opening which the Indians called a cave, and by which they said one could reach Mexico in an hour. I crawled under and found a pointed arch roof formed by stones overlapping each other, but was prevented from exploring further by want of light, and the Padre's crying out to me that it was the season for earthquakes; and he laughed more than usual at the hurry with which I came out.

Stevens also indicated that the Indians in another village, Ocosingo, had a traditional story about a subterranean way connecting with the old city of Palenque, some 150 miles away.

Recent finds in the Americas tend to substantiate these ancient legends rather than discredit them. A vast underground labyrinth called the Loltun Cave System has been found under the Puuc Hills in Yucatan. It contains pillars of rock carved into idols of grotesque shape. According to the findings of the archaeologists, these hoary specimens date back some 10000 years.

In *Gold of the Gods* Erich von Daniken relates how he met an Argentinian explorer who has discovered a system of ancient tunnels, hitherto known only to the Indians, which run for many miles under the wild jungle of Ecuador. This lone adventurer, Juan Moricz, was researching the area bounded by the rivers Zamora, Santiago and Yuapa during 1965, when he stumbled on the cave entrance at the bottom of a 700-foot shaft. von Daniken recounts his subsequent trek with Moricz into the depths of these caves which, he insists, are man-made and contain a vast amount of ancient gold artifacts. In particular, he describes seeing a 'library' of inscribed plates made out of a metal which he could not identify. Consisting partly of plaques and partly of leaves only millimetres thick, the plates bore many strange hieroglyphics. He also states that Moricz allowed him to see, but not to photograph, many of the beautifully worked, solid gold articles stored in the tunnels. He has, however, included in his book photographs of gold and silver artifacts located in a nearby mission and said to have been brought out of the tunnels by the Indians.

Von Daniken also quotes at length the startling findings of an expedition mounted in Peru in 1971, who based their search on information left by Pizarro himself.

During the conquest of the New World, the Spaniards discovered strange cave entrances sealed with huge slabs of stone, on Huascaran, the Mountain of the Incas, and although they strongly suspected that storerooms lay behind, they apparently failed to gain entry. The brief reference to the caves lay forgotten in the archives until 1971, when speleologists of the expedition decided to attempt verification of the tale.

The explorers, equipped with all the latest technical devices, arrived in the neighbourhood of the Peruvian village of Otuzco and after removing the rocks which sealed the entrance, descended into the caves. At the 200-foot level the team made a staggering discovery. At the far end of the caves, which had several storeys, they found themselves confronted by watertight doors made out of gigantic slabs of rock. In spite of the tremendous weight, it was found that four men could push open the giant doors, and they were able to see that each door cunningly pivoted on a stone ball laid in a bed formed by dripping water. The discoverers subsequently described a vast tunnel lying beyond the doors, of such dimensions as would make a modern underground constructor green with envy.

The tunnel led straight towards the coast on the west side of the Andes, at times with an extremely steep slope, yet with a flooring of stone that was pitted and grooved in order to make it slip-proof. After traversing a distance of nearly sixty-five miles, the tunnel finally disappeared into pitch-black sea-water. It was assumed that, in times past, the subterranean way continued until it reached the island of Guanape lying just off the coast of Peru at this point, but that more recent volcanic activity had in some way breached the tunnel wall, allowing the Pacific Ocean to seep in.

These recent revelations, it can be seen, go a considerable way towards supporting the strange legend reported by Madame Blavatsky more than one hundred years earlier. If there are huge, obviously engineered rock doors in the Huascaran caves, there may really exist a 'Tomb of the Incas' with similarly designed doors. And the legendary treasure of the Incas may really be stored away awaiting discovery by some intrepid adventurer.

A Scots engineer and amateur archaeologist, Stanley Hall, avidly read *Gold of the Gods*, wherein von Daniken claimed to have seen with his own eyes a treasure house of gold secreted in the tunnels. So fired was he with enthusiasm that he organized an expedition to the Ecuadorian cave system. Scientists from the Universities of Edinburgh and Quito shared his enthusiasm, and he gained still more support from the British and Ecuadorian armies. The final complement of the expedition boasted thirty-five British Army personnel, twenty Ecuadorian soldiers, ten university experts, a nurse, a medical researcher and an ornithologist. As an added bonus, the famous astronaut Neil Armstrong agreed to accompany them.

In August 1976 the expedition forced its way up the raging torrent of the Santiago in their small inflatable rubber boats to reach the mouth of the 700-foot shaft.

Subsequent pictures brought back by the team show the enormous rock chambers of the cave system – natural shafts in the limestone strata, not man-made as claimed by von Daniken. Masks and pottery fragments found in the twelve miles of the caves covered by the team date back to about 1000 BC – but of the golden treasure, there was no sign, despite a diligent two-month search by the members of the expedition.

One more small item of evidence is relevant to the story of the great tunnels of Peru. The tale, a self-contained treasure legend on its own, begins in 1904, when the Lord Cowdray Mining Company of London engaged a man to do some prospecting for them in the gold-bearing hills of California. The man called himself J. C. Brown, although there is some doubt as to whether this was his real name. He was an experienced man, forty-nine years old.

Ranging north from the gold country lying north-east of

Sacramento, he struck into the Cascade Mountains until he reached an almost inaccessible and remote area, miles from the nearest human habitation. Here, in the side of a mountain, he accidentally discovered signs of a landslide, not of recent

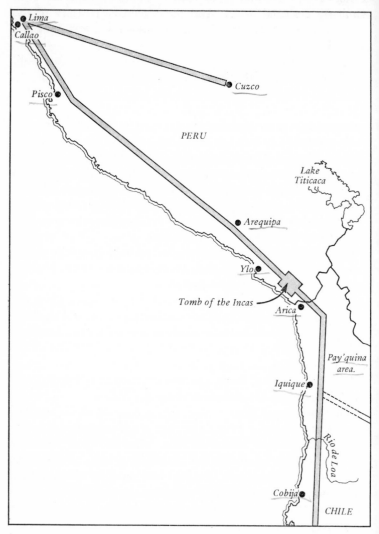

A map of the tunnel and tomb.

origin, and at once gave his attention to studying the geological formation. To his amazement, he stumbled on the mouth of a tunnel that seemed to be man-made. He cleared the entrance and followed the tunnel down until it opened out into a long narrow room, the walls of which were lined with tempered copper, and hung with shields and wall-pieces made of gold. In his opinion, the dimensions of the room were too precise to be of natural origin. Exploring further, he found in one corner of the room a stack of thin gold plates that had strange hieroglyphics on each side.

The inevitable conclusion is that there may be more in Madame Blavatsky's story than meets the eye. Her plan of the tunnel and Tomb is extant. Of course, it must be realized that she gathered her information in 1851, and since then changes have taken place in the boundary lines of Bolivia and Peru. Bolivia no longer extends down to the sea, and the area of the three peaks is now to be found in Chile. The boundary between Chile and Peru is several hundred miles further north.

Harold Wilkins investigated the legend of the tunnel in 1940 and found that the Pay'quina mentioned in Madame Blavatsky's account is not a river as she describes, but an area on the Rio de Loa, two hundred miles south of Arica. It is here that the three peaks are situated. On her actual plan of the tunnel Madame Blavatsky notes ' . . . Pay'quina, and in this

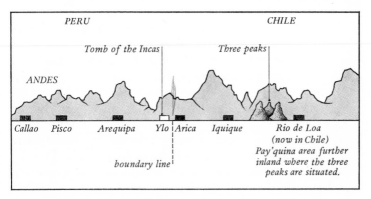

The outline of the coast copied from Madame Blavatsky's own map but updated in accordance with modern boundaries.

part are three hills in a triangle (a continuation of the Andes). In one of these hills, I forget which one, about halfway up is the door to the end of the tunnel.'

Wilkins also made it clear that the rock called the Tomb of the Incas is situated in a little bay about 100 miles north of Arica, called Ylo. According to the legend, the tomb intersecting the tunnel is deep under this rock. The mysterious hieroglyphics carved in bas-relief on this rock were noted down by Madame Blavatsky and reproduced on her map. According to Wilkins, the southern end of the tunnel peters out somewhere in the region of the Atacama desert, some nine hundred miles from Lima!

Madame Blavatsky's mysterious Peruvian pointed out that 'the mere task of purifying the mephitic air of the tunnel, which had not been entered for centuries, would be a serious one'. However, this does not seem to be the case, for Erich von Daniken reports that the system of tunnels in Ecuador was adequately ventilated.

The technical care with which the tunnel system was planned is proved by the ventilation shafts that occur at regular intervals. These shafts are all accurately worked and on an average, are between five feet ten inches, and ten feet long, by two feet seven inches wide. Swarms of buzzard-like birds leave the dark labyrinth through these shafts, coming and going all day long, and finally returning to die in the dungeon.

Here then, is a method that suggests itself for finding Madame Blavatsky's tunnel. Assuming that the tunnel is routed near the rock at Arica, the so-called Tomb of the Incas, I would imagine that the habits of the birds in the area would repay study. A possible entry could be made if one of the ventilation shafts were located.

It only remains for us to speculate that, if some lucky individual were to effect an entry into the legendary shaft, would he find awaiting him a fortune in Inca gold?

One last word regarding the age and origin of these tunnels. The Inca period was said to have lasted about three hundred years, starting in the early 1200s, and it is agreed by experts that no known form of writing was used by them. Therefore the hieroglyphics said to have been carved on the temple at Cuzco, and the similar markings at Arica, were not of Inca origin, but must have been the last traces left by a much earlier race – as were the tunnels. When this race existed it is not yet possible to determine, but I would like to record one interesting and related discovery.

One of the photographic plates in von Daniken's book shows a stele of solid gold, said to have been recovered from the nearby tunnel system. It is covered with a number of hieroglyphics which have been hammered into the surface of the inch-and-a-half thick plate. I have found that some of the symbols compare favourably with those found depicted in a treatise on magic called *The Key of Solomon the King*, which has been compiled from ancient Hebrew manuscripts now in the British Museum. The book gives a table of characters that are said to comprise an ancient form of secret writing called Malachim, or the Writing of the Angels. This is a form of Celestial Writing, the characters of which are made by joining star positions with lines. I hasten to add that only two out of fifty-six characters on the stele make this comparison, but even that small amount seems interesting. Lastly, the first of the characters that Madame Blavatsky reported as carved on the Arica rock, thus: ⌞• is exactly similar to the cipher of the letter Aleph, found in the Jewish Cabala, which dates from biblical times. According to this book, Aleph has the value of one; and signifies an Ox.

'President' Walker's
Forgotten Gold

William Walker was born of rich parents on 8 May 1824 in Nashville, Tennessee. His father, a banker from Edinburgh, had emigrated to America and married a girl from one of the aristocratic Southern families, settling on a plantation nearby. Growing up, Walker graduated from the University of Nashville, and went on to Edinburgh Medical College to become a physician. He was a short, slim, man weighing about nine and a half stone with a reserved but restless nature. When he passed out of the College, instead of going back to the United States to practise, he travelled in Europe, spending two years studying law.

Walker eventually returned to America and set up as a physician in Philadelphia, where he first attracted public attention by duelling with William Hix Graham, a prominent local figure. This incident gives some indication of the character that was being formed. The duellists exchanged shots, with no apparent hit on either man, and the seconds were about to give the signal for another round when one of them noticed a pool of blood at Walker's feet. On examination, it was found that he had received a wound in the foot but had tried to conceal the fact by using his other foot to cover it with sand, thereby gaining another shot. Agreeing that the men's honour had been satisfied, the seconds called off the duel.

Soon after this incident, Walker left Philadelphia and changed from medicine to law, which he practised in his home town of Nashville for a short time. He was, however, too restless to enjoy the day-to-day routine of a lawyer, and moved on to New

Orleans where he became a journalist on the *New Orleans Crescent*. In 1850, he moved again, this time to San Francisco, where he became the editor of the *San Francisco Herald*.

Walker wielded a vitriolic pen when writing his editorials and this soon gained him a number of enemies. He fought at least three duels, killing the first two challengers and outstaring the third until he received an apology. When he was twenty-eight years old an Indian massacre occurred on the Arizona–Mexican border, in which American settler families were killed. In his editorials in the *Herald* Walker took the opportunity to express some novel ideas.

A comparatively small body of determined Americans might gain a position on the Sonora frontier and protect the families on the border from the Indians, and such an act would be one of humanity whether or not sanctioned by the Mexican Government.

The condition of the upper part of Sonora is a disgrace to the civilization of the continent and the people of the United States are immediately responsible before the world for this and other Apache outrages.

He went on to point out that the Apaches were allowed to run wild in Sonora, and finished the editorial by stating:

The state of this region furnishes the best defense for any American intending to settle there without the formal consent of Mexico; and, although political changes will certainly follow the establishment of a colony, they may be justified by the plea that any social organization, no matter how secure is preferable to that in which individuals and families are altogether at the mercy of brutal savages.

This idea seemed to take hold of Walker and he set out to practise what he preached. The first step was to form a business partnership with an influential banker, Henry P. Watkins, who raised the necessary funds to organize an expedition. Walker then opened a recruiting office to enlist a force of forty-five men. At that time there were a considerable number of footloose, adventurous types in San Francisco, ranging from unsuccessful gold miners to ex-bandits and rustlers. Walker found the response to his call for an army much greater than he had expected and promptly enlarged his plans, deciding to send, not one, but two invading armies into Mexico.

In October 1853 Walker and forty-five hand-picked men sailed out of San Francisco in the small barque *Caroline*. They left at night, to avoid the US marshals who had orders not to permit the ship to leave the harbour, and, gaining the open sea, they sailed southwards along the coast down the narrow neck of land known as Baja California. On 28 October they reached the small port of Cape San Lucas, on the southernmost tip of this neck of land, and there they dropped anchor, rowed ashore and took over the village without a shot being fired.

After a short stay, the *Caroline* continued round the cape, turning northwards for a short distance until the town of La Paz was reached. Walker had expected some resistance at this point, but he found that he was able to lead his men into the town unopposed. His first act was to make the Governor, Francisco Espanosa, a prisoner of war, an event which evoked complete indifference from the citizens of La Paz. Walker found that the Federal government had recently lost patience at Espanosa's frequent drunken carousals and another Governor was already on his way from Mexico to replace him.

Three days after Walker and his company had occupied La Paz, the new Governor, Colonel Carlos Robollero, arrived, only to be clapped in gaol along with Espanosa. Elated with his success, Walker sent a message to Watkins back in San Francisco.

Events proceed as planned. I have formed a government upon a firm and sure basis. I have appointed ten of my own men to fill the chief offices: civil, military and naval. The others I have made first citizens of Sonora as there are not enough offices to go round. By the time you receive this I will have become president of a larger Republic of Sonora comprising both the State of this name and the State of Lower California.

While Walker had been undertaking the capture of La Paz, the second phase of his operation had been implemented. More than three hundred of the volunteer recruits had trekked overland from San Francisco and crossed the border into Baja California, where they descended on the town of San Vincente, some ninety miles south of the US border. This force, under the command of a thirty-eight-year-old Texan stagecoach robber, Gary Fraser, was to wait for Walker's expedition to march north from La Paz to meet them, once they had captured the town.

At that time, San Vincente was being used as a depot for shipments of gold extracted from the vast mines in Sonora. In an effort to foil the Apache Indians, who had made a business of attacking and looting the mule trains of gold on their way to Mexico City, the loads of precious metal were being re-routed to San Vincente and taken by boat to Nicaragua, thence going overland to their destination by a circuitous route. When Fraser and his force captured the town, they discovered the vast shipments of gold awaiting transport. Attacking the freight depot and killing three guards, they seized some £500 000 in gold. At this point, losing interest in Walker and his plans of conquest, Fraser had begun to think about returning to the US with the looted gold. He and a few other unsavoury characters including a close friend, a gunslinger from Arizona, plotted to blow up the gold store and make a night-time getaway.

On 28 November Walker arrived in San Vincente and soon found out what was afoot. He acted swiftly. Accusing Fraser and his friend of conspiracy and treason against the government of Sonora, he court-martialled them. In fifteen minutes they were found guilty, marched out to the public square and shot. Two more of Fraser's desperado friends were stripped to the waist, flogged and then driven from the city.

With the execution of Fraser, Walker began to display traits of unbending command which, according to the historian James Jeffrey Roche, 'made his name a word of terror in the ears of men who feared nothing else, human or divine'. He assembled his remaining men and divided them into two groups. From one he was certain of loyalty. The other he ordered to stack their arms, and then he addressed them. He informed them that it was his intention to march overland around the head of the Gulf of California and into Sonora, pointing out that they would be forced to fight dangerous Indians on the way as well as the pitched battles that would ensue when they engaged the soldiers of the Mexican army. He told them of the hardships of the terrain over which they would be marching and fighting, a savage and inhospitable prospect. In conclusion, Walker invited the men who wished to join him on this proposed expedition to step forward. Most had been looking forward to dividing up the captured gold and heading back to the United States. Now they were starkly aware of Walker's determination to see his plan through. Disillusioned and discouraged by the grim description of what was in store for them, only forty-one stepped forward.

Walker stripped those who did not volunteer of all weapons and marched them to the northern edge of the town. There he gave each man a small supply of food and water and set him on the trail towards the US border. He indicated that if any of them attempted to return to San Vincente, they would be shot on sight. This threat amounted to a death sentence, for the men would be forced to march unarmed over a hundred miles of desert country infested with hostile savages. Only a few in fact ever made it to the border; the rest died from hunger and thirst or at the hands of the Indians.

Walker confiscated the captured shipment of gold, announcing that it would form the basis of a public treasury as soon as a permanent capital city was established for his new republic. By March 1854 everything was ready. Walker and his hand-picked army of eighty-six men marched eastwards, accompanied by a long mule train carrying arms, ammunition, food and water – and, of course, the gold. In four days, they reached and annexed the small village of Valle San Pablo, and then marched on.

Several miles beyond this village, Walker called a halt. Ahead of them, he knew, was a wild region, extremely difficult to cross. To make the going easier he gave the order to cache about three hundred spare rifles and a large amount of ammunition. These were hidden in some caves, and the gold then redistributed to make each mule's load lighter.

Continuing on their way, the army reached the Colorado River at a point above the place where it empties into the Gulf of California. Here, the men spent about four days salvaging drifting logs to make rafts for the crossing. Walker was considerably worried at this stage, because the river, lazy and placid to all appearances, was subject to sudden, wild surges of current – or so he had been warned. But his luck held and the crossing was made without loss.

Once over the Colorado, the army headed southwards into the hills, but here Walker's good fortune seemed to wane. They were repeatedly attacked by hostile bands of Yaqui and Apache Indians, who were driven off by rifle fire, but not before inflicting some casualties. Then, as they traversed the mountains and approached the harsh terrain of the Gran Desierto, they encountered a strong force of Mexican Federalistas. After a series of savage engagements, they repulsed the Mexicans, but a more deadly, silent enemy was now attacking them – disease.

Few or no medical supplies were available; soon the wounded were becoming infected and dying for lack of treatment. The 'President' of Sonora's army was reduced to fifty men.

At a council of war it was decided to return to San Vincente. As they re-crossed the hills, the Mexican soldiers remained close to their flanks, cutting down the stragglers and nearly annihilating the whole force in a gorge 'which widened out at the middle to a plateau of half a mile across, with a narrow opening at each end'. This gorge becomes important as a clue in the location of the treasure cache.

They fought their way out of the gorge, only to find that Indians were attacking from either flank, but the quick-witted commander resorted to a trick which set the Indians to flight, and led his men to the safety of a further defile. By this time, however, Walker's army numbered only thirty-five and the Mexican force of 250 well-trained troops was hot on their heels.

That evening, they pitched camp on top of a narrow mountain pass overlooking the Gran Desierto. Some way below could be seen the fires of the Mexican troops. Walker's plan was to retreat to San Vincente and there to join up with a strong reinforcing army from San Francisco. In the meantime, the gold had become a drag on them, so it was decided to cache it on the spot and return later to recover it. With the load lightened, they would stand a far better chance of making fast time to the Colorado River and crossing before either the Indians or the Federalistas overran them. During the night, therefore, the consignment of gold, still in the pack-saddles, was unloaded and concealed in shallow clefts in the side of the rocky pass. It seems unlikely that the treasure was buried, for a pile of newly turned earth would certainly have attracted the attention of the pursuing Mexicans. As far as can be determined, the openings of the clefts or caves were camouflaged with boulders arranged in the most natural manner possible. Walker and his remaining men fully intended to return with a larger army to reclaim the treasure, and therefore did not attempt to make the cache more permanent, nor was any map made of the location, each man committing the spot to memory. Before dawn on the following morning, Walker led his men out of the mountain and down towards the Colorado River, taking the mule trains with them.

He knew that by this time the Mexican government would have been informed of the looting of the gold bullion from San Vincente, and therefore assumed that the pursuing Mexican commander knew also. By taking the mule train away from the site of the cache, he hoped to deceive the Mexicans into thinking that the gold was still packed on them. In the mid-morning, he stampeded one of the mule trains into the desolate *mesa*. The animals made off, leaving their tracks in the soft ground. At noon, he stampeded the remaining train. By means of this ruse, he hoped to induce the Mexicans to pause long enough to give him and his men time to cross the river.

Towards sunset that day, they reached the Colorado and re-crossed the river on the rafts which they had used coming out. Safe at last, they made camp for the night, the half-starved men dining on fish from the river.

Several days later, they reached San Vincente. It was now six weeks since Walker had set out, but still no reinforcements had arrived from San Francisco. His reception by the people of San Vincente was hardly cordial since the politically powerful owners of the shipment that Walker had taken were attempting to force the Mexican government to levy a tax on the town's citizens as restitution for the loss.

Making camp on the outskirts of the city, Walker attempted to find a boat big enough to get him and his men back to San Francisco, but he met with no success. The Mexican commander, Colonel Melendrez, was advancing on the city and Walker realized that he would be trapped if he stayed.

The only course left was to set out on foot on the long trek to the US border, taking the same route to which Walker had condemned the less loyal of his followers, weeks before. They moved steadily over the trail, keeping in a tight, determined little band as a deterrent to the raiding Indians. On 6 May they reached a point just a few miles south of the border and camped for the night. But, as darkness fell, they were shocked to see a number of camp-fires ahead of them and Walker bitterly realized why there had been no sign of pursuit by the Mexicans. The wily colonel's Apache scouts had known of a quicker route across the desert and he was now in a position three miles below the border, blocking their escape to US soil.

In the morning, Colonel Melendrez sent an emissary to Walker asking for his surrender in what appeared to be a hopeless predicament. Walker refused, deciding to try the same ruse that he had successfully employed against the Indians in the gorge. Placing his second-in-command and six men in ambush behind some rocks overlooking the camp, he pretended to retreat southwards with the rest of his little band. Melendrez was completely taken in and gave the order to advance.

The Mexican troops were met by a withering fire from the ambush, at which Walker and his party turned quickly about and charged. Caught by surprise, the Mexicans fled in all directions and by the time Melendrez had reformed his men, Walker and his group, with the exception of one casualty, were safely over the border. According to Roche, 'Four and thirty tattered, hungry, gaunt pedestrians, whimsically representing in their persons the president, cabinet, army and navy of Sonora, marched across the line and surrendered as prisoners of war to Major McKinstry, USA. It was the 8th day of May 1854; and so Walker kept his 30th birthday.'

Walker's army was tried for breaking the neutrality of the United States, but was acquitted. Tired but not the least bit discouraged, Walker considered mounting a second expedition to go and recover the gold, but reluctantly abandoned the idea on the advice of his financial backers.

In fact he never did return to recover the cache. One year

later, he and some of the men who had returned with him set out for Nicaragua where Walker was made Commanding General to the Nicaraguan army. Later he realized his ambition and was made President of the Republic, but like so many of the revolutionary regimes of the period, his government was eventually overthrown. In September 1860, at the age of thirty-six, he was executed by a firing squad.

History records that not all of the men present at the burial of the cache went to Nicaragua with Walker. But, having stirred up a hornets' nest, it is unlikely that any of the survivors made an attempt to recover the treasure. With the Mexican army scouring the area and hostile Indians a constant threat, no small expedition would stand a chance of getting across the rough country without suffering hunger. Any party would be forced to take a large amount of provisions, and by enlarging the expedition increase the risk of being observed. There is no known report of Colonel Melendrez backtracking and finding the cache and it seems that Walker's ruse was successful.

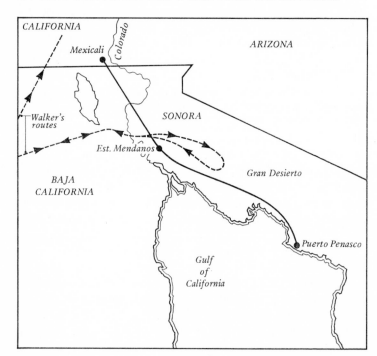

According to Roche's account of the expedition, the gold was put in the caves which were situated in a narrow pass to the south of which was the *mesa* of the Gran Desierto. Half a day's ride to the south was the gorge mentioned earlier, in which Walker and his men narrowly escaped annihilation by the Indians. The site of the gold cache was one full day's ride from the Colorado River, in a southerly direction.

Nowadays there is a main railway line which runs from Mexicali, on the border, down to Puerto Penasco. One of the stops on this line is the Est. Mendanos, which must be the nearest point to this hidden cache.

The Caches of Le Vasseur and L'Estang

At the beginning of the eighteenth century the Indian Ocean, encompassing the island of Mauritius and as far as the Seychelles, was infested with pirates, many of whom had sought refuge there after their great exodus from Tortuga. They were merciless robbers who, under the skull and crossbones, hunted ruthlessly all over the ocean. It may be remembered that Captain Kidd was commissioned to go there in 1695 to clear them out, but instead himself found rich pickings.

While the era lasted, the pirate gangs did very well, living like lords in their secret hideouts, and caching their booty in many places among the scattering of islands. Often, they were forced to run, leaving the treasure caches uncollected and, in the end, English and French warships hunted them like vermin until they were wiped out. One of the last of these buccaneers was Olivier le Vasseur, better known as 'La Buze' ('The Buzzard').

In the 1720s Le Vasseur is said to have joined forces with another pirate, a former lieutenant of the Royal Navy named John Taylor, and between them they accumulated a sizable amount of stolen loot. In 1721 they caught the Portuguese ship *Vierge du Cap* as she sailed from the harbour at St Denis, Réunion (then called Bourbon Island). Having captured and boarded her, Le Vasseur and Taylor were delighted to find a large cargo of rich treasure in her hold. They split the loot and used the captured ship for further pirating. Le Vasseur sailed to Mahé in the Seychelles shortly after, and it is thought that there, in an underground cavern, he deposited a large part of his booty.

The following year he retired from piracy to settle on the island of Ste Marie. Soon after, the King of France declared an amnesty for all pirates, but Le Vasseur spurned the offer because the main condition was the voluntary return of all stolen booty.

In 1730 Le Vasseur, who had been working as a pilot in the Bay of Antongil, Madagascar, came out of his retirement to command the *Victorieux*. One story says that while at work, he was recognized by a French naval officer, and so forced to return to his former ways. Whatever the case, his comeback was short-lived, for he was engaged and captured by Captain L'Ermmitte of the French ship, *Méduse*, off Fort Dauphin, Madagascar. L'Ermmitte boarded Le Vasseur's ship and hanged all the pirates. La Buze himself was taken in chains back to gaol on Bourbon Isle.

On 7 July 1730 the notorious pirate was publicly hanged; as he mounted to the scaffold, he threw a piece of paper at the watching crowd, crying, 'My treasure to he who can understand!' It is not known for certain whether this dramatic scene actually took place, but fortunately, it makes no difference to the story of his cache. In the years that followed, the paper left by Le Vasseur has been variously described as a map and a cryptogram, and only one fact is clear: the original has long since gone and only copies remain. Some of these can be found in the archives of Mahé, Mauritius and Paris, and consist of eight documents in all. Not all relate solely to Le Vasseur, because seventy years after his death his buried cache became connected with that of 'Butin', 'The Loot'.

At the end of the eighteenth century, a different type of privateer had appeared in the Indian Ocean. Known as 'corsairs', these men carried commissions from the French government, now at war with England, to destroy all British shipping. Equipped with fast vessels, the corsairs preyed heavily on the English merchantmen. From their base in Mauritius they successfully ran the blockade mounted by English warships and inflicted a heavy toll on the merchantmen of the East India Company.

Butin's real name was Bernadin Nageon de L'Estang – a good name for a corsair since it means 'Sailor of the Waters'.

L'Estang had established a home base in Mauritius, then known as Île de France, and, during this period, he either buried several caches of his own, or assumed ownership of caches left by Le Vasseur. Perhaps he did both. The translation of the surviving documents certainly indicates that he had in his possession Le Vasseur's cryptogram.

[Letter from] Butin Nageon de L'Estang to his nephew Justin Marius, 20 Floréal year VIII [10 May 1800].

My dear Justin, should death overcome me before we meet, a faithful friend will hand over to you my will and my documents. I urge you to follow my instructions and carry out my last wishes and God will bless you.

Get our influential friends to send you to the Indian Ocean and go to the spot on the Île de France indicated in my will. Climb the eastward cliff; taking twenty-five or thirty paces east, according to the documents, there you will find pirates' signs to help you trace out a circle, of which the stream is a few paces from the centre. The treasure is there. By a peculiar combination, the figures of the cryptogram yield the name B.N. at this point.

I have lost many documents in a shipwreck; I have already removed several treasures; only four remain, buried in the same manner by the same pirates, which you will find by the key to the combinations and the other papers which you will receive at the same time.

The second treasure on the Île de France lies to the north of the former, with similar markings. By tracing out a circle at this spot, and following the instructions, you will come upon it as upon that of Rodriguez.

The second document contains L'Estang's will:

I am departing to join the ranks in defence of my country. As I will most probably be killed, I am drawing up my will and give to my nephew Jean Marius Nageon de L'Estang, officer in the reserve, to wit:

My land bordering the La Chaux stream at Grand Port [Île de France] and the treasures rescued from the *Indus*, to wit:

I foundered in a creek near Vacoas. I went upstream and deposited in a cave the valuables from the *Indus* and there marked B.N., my name. I have taken the precautions of making my writings difficult to read; I will explain everything to Justin if I meet him.

The third is a letter to his beloved brother, Etienne.

My dearest brother, I have been ill since we took Tamatave, in spite of the care of my friend the Commandant. I am weak and the fear of death is upon me, I am speaking to you for the last time, dear Etienne, and impart to you my last wishes.

When I am dead, Commandant Hamon will send on to you what little I now possess and have saved during my adventurous life as a sailor. You know, dear Etienne, that my life's dream has been to build up a fortune to restore the splendour of our house. With the good-will the First Consul has shown me after a glorious feat of arms, I should have managed to do so. But, as God will not permit me to carry out this duty and I feel death approaching, swear to me, dear Etienne, to carry out my wish.

In the course of my adventurous life, before embarking on the *Apollo*, I was a member of the pirate band which did so much damage to Spain and our enemies, the English. We made some fine captures together, but during our last fight with a large English frigate off the coast of Hindustan, our captain was wounded and, on his death bed, confided to me his secrets and papers for finding the sizeable treasures buried in the Indian Ocean.

After first making sure that I was a Freemason, he asked me to sue them to arm pirate ships against the English. But I was weary of this wanderer's life and preferred to enroll as a regular and wait till France was at peace to find these treasures and return home. Swear to me that your elder son will realize my dream and use this fortune one day to restore our house.

The Commandant will hand over to you the writings about the treasures. There are three. The one buried on my beloved Île de France is sizeable. As stated in the writings you will see: three iron casks and large jars full of minted doubloons and bullion worth thirty million and a casket, crammed with diamonds from the Visapour and Golconda mines.

The letters were accompanied by two cryptograms giving the locations of the caches. One begins: 'As a first mark a stone of PGT. Take the second V of this. There make S north for a cubit in the same way. . . .'

The second begins: 'Take N-North 48 degrees South B- 78 paces 4 degrees south . . .' Also included was the cryptogram reproduced at the end of this chapter.

Somehow, copies of these documents have survived and, while no treasure has been reported found on Mauritius, one of Butin's treasure caches was unearthed in 1916 on the island

of Pemba, off Zanzibar. It was recognizable by the initials
B.N. carved in the rock.

The Indian Ocean is a cyclone area and often suffers violent
weather conditions comparable to the hurricanes of the Caribbean. In 1923 a violent storm passed over Mahé island in the
Seychelles, wreaking its usual havoc. When it had blown
itself out, a woman resident went down to the shore of her Bel
Ombre beach home in the north-west of the island, and was
intrigued to find that the storm had exposed some strange
carvings on the rocks. Madame Savy, whose land it was, was
aware of the pirate traditions connected with the area and so
began to investigate. She found sculptured rocks representing
dogs, horses, snakes, a young woman, a tortoise, hearts, an urn,
a man's head and a large, staring eye.

When this news was made public, a notary living nearby

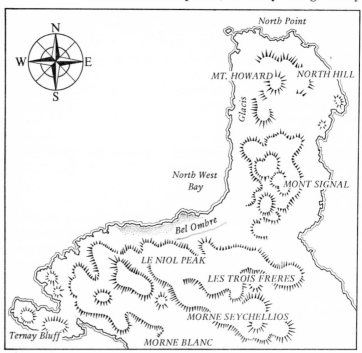

*The northern part of Mahé Island. The workings of Cruise-Wilkins,
who discovered the markings on the rocks here, are illustrated
opposite page 96.*

came immediately to see Madame Savy, disclosing that, for
some time, he had been in possession of documents relating to a
pirate treasure. One of the papers mentioned a horse, a dog,
a young woman and an eye, as part of the directions for location
of the cache. These consisted of the two letters and the will
written by L'Estang; the cryptogram in Masonic cipher; a
paper on which was inscribed four magical or astrological
characters; and a cryptogram which began: 'Take the second,
go with it close by pqtx then choose L 4 VL f SN 2 Close the
same. . . .' Until Madame Savy's discovery, these had meant
nothing to the notary, but he now concluded that they could
only refer to the beach at Bel Ombre.

Accordingly, they began a series of searches and soon came
on some grisly remains. Close to the carving of the eye two
coffins were found, their rotting contents identified as pirates'
bodies by the ear-rings attached to the bodies. Close by was
another corpse, interred without ceremony. But although
Madame Savy and the notary spent many hours digging and
poring over the documents, they could not solve the mystery
of the treasure island.

In 1948 a former Grenadier Guardsman, Reginal Cruise-
Wilkins, a sufferer from malaria, came to Mahé from Kenya to
convalesce. He had originally intended to stay for only three
weeks but found that he was unable to get a ship back to
Mombasa for some three months. Accordingly, he rented a
bungalow at Beau Vellon beach, not far from Bel Ombre.
Soon he became acquainted with the legend of the treasure and,
for the want of something to do, copied out the documents and
began to try and solve the puzzle. After a preliminary examination, he became much more interested and spent, at one point,
eighteen hours a day working on them.

After a few weeks, everybody was stunned when he announced that he had almost solved the mystery. In 1949 he
went to Nairobi to raise the financial backing necessary for an
organized search. A syndicate of backers was formed and the
Seychelles authorities were interested enough to supply
manpower. Cruise-Wilkins imported a professional mineral
diviner who gave the opinion that there was treasure buried
under some twenty feet of solid granite.

Working with the documents, bearings were taken from marks and carving on the rocks, and six of them were found to intersect at a certain point, beneath which Cruise-Wilkins assumed the treasure cavern to be located. He fenced off the site and the native labourers began to dig.

Soon they uncovered what appeared to be a roughly hewn staircase, mentioned in the documents, which led upwards from the underground cavern to the huge dome of rock that over-looks Bel Ombre beach. There were crude carvings cut into the staircase wall, but the entrance to the cavern was blocked, either by natural subsidence, or deliberately.

At first Cruise-Wilkins was confident that blasting would open the cave, but it was found that the method of concealment was far more sophisticated than he had supposed. As time went by, he gradually formed the theory that it was based on stories from Greek mythology and on the position of the stars. He discovered a carving of Andromeda chained to the Ethiopian coast, waiting to be devoured by the sea monster, and also reached the conclusion that the puzzle was laid out over sixty acres. In order to reach the treasure, he thought, it was necessary to perform the Twelve Labours of Hercules, set out in twelve distinct spheres. For example, the task given to Hercules of killing the water-snake, the Hydra, would have its parallel in the need to divert an underground stream away from the treasure cave.

Visiting Mahé in 1967 the author Athol Thomas was interested enough in the progress of the hunt to devote a chapter of his book *Forgotten Eden* to it. He found that Cruise-Wilkins had invested in the hunt, over the intervening sixteen years, some £9700 of his own money, plus another £24000 supplied by his backers. He had performed the Twelve Labours – and others besides, including the removal piece by piece of 700 tons of rock from a granite shelf to reveal what he considered to be significant carvings.

The beach had been found to be honeycombed with man-made tunnels in which other finds relative to the myths were found. Three round stones (the Golden Apples) and a piece of willow pattern (mentioned in the documents) came to light, along with the blade of a sword (identified as the scimitar of

Perseus), sticks placed upright in the floor of a cave (perhaps to represent the dragon's teeth planted by Jason), and near an underground stream, a coin of Le Vasseur's time (payment to Charon for ferrying the dead across the Styx). Cruise-Wilkins had located the cavern where the treasure lay and was convinced that it would have to be approached from the north – any other direction would invite disaster, as Le Vasseur had set many traps. The treasure, he believed, was in three chests each seven feet long by three feet wide. During the extent of the hunt he had been visited by the BBC, the *London Illustrated News* and by the Russian news agency Tass.

Connecting the Le Vasseur treasure to Greek mythology is not such a fanciful idea as one may first think. In fact, the story of Hercules' entry to the Underworld readily lends itself to the burial of treasure, and investigation indicates that it does indeed fit many of the finds made by Cruise-Wilkins. Of course, this is speculation; we must return to basic facts. It seems apparent from Butin's letters that he inherited Le Vasseur's caches, and the one point that must be borne in mind is that Butin specifically stated that he 'removed several treasures; only four remain'. In the third letter he tells of the secret papers handed over to him and then states: 'There are three [treasures].' This seems to indicate that the first treasure, which is buried in a cave upstream from the creek near Vacoas, is his own and not Le Vasseur's. This creek is nowadays called the Poudre d'Or and in 1951 F. D. Ommanney reports being taken there to see the remaining pirate markings.

The other three, then, must consist of, first, the cache in the north of Mauritius, probably in the Belmont area where there are known to be pirate markings; secondly, the cache that Butin indicates to be buried on the island of Rodriguez; thirdly, the cache at Bel Ombre. But there is one snag: one of Butin's treasures was unearthed on Pemba. Therefore it is conceivable that one of the other three locations may have already been visited by Butin and the treasure removed. We do not know which one.

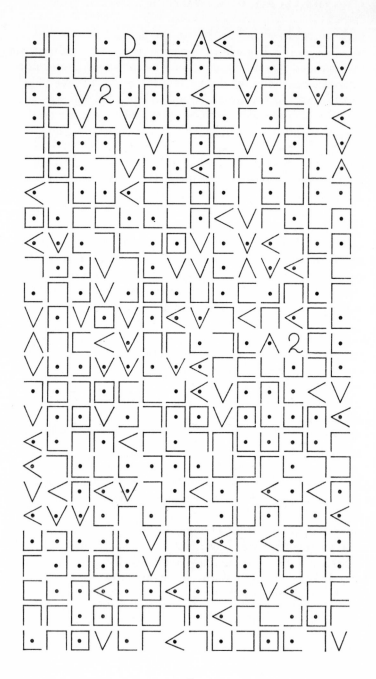

58

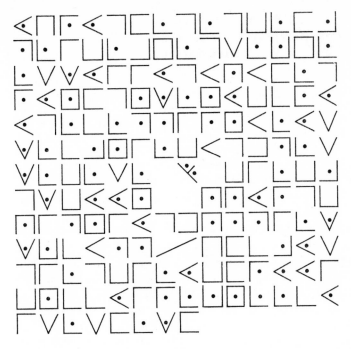

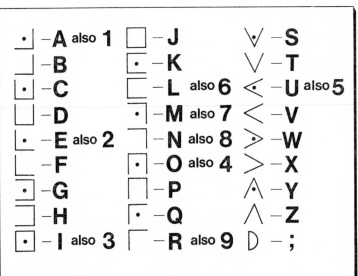

⌐· –**A** also **1**	☐ –**J**	∨· –**S**	
⌐⌐ –**B**	⌐· –**K**	∨ –**T**	
⌐· –**C**	⌐ –**L** also **6**	≪ –**U** also **5**	
⊔ –**D**	·⌐ –**M** also **7**	≪ –**V**	
⌐· –**E** also **2**	⌐ –**N** also **8**	≫ –**W**	
⌐ –**F**	·⌐ –**O** also **4**	≫ –**X**	
·⌐ –**G**	⌐ –**P**	∧ –**Y**	
⌐⌐ –**H**	⌐· –**Q**	∧ –**Z**	
·⌐ –**I** also **3**	⌐ –**R** also **9**	ⅅ –**;**	

One of Le Vasseur's cryptograms was enciphered by the old Royal Arch Masons' and Rosicrucians' method. It is an ancient and simple form, and the key is as follows.

The message required is then enciphered by using part of the square or cross to represent the letters, either with or without a dot. Thus A = ⌐· , B = ⌐⌐ , and so on.

Decipherment of the document hardly helps because it is sprinkled with mis-spellings, anagrams and spare letters. Robert Charroux, in his book *Treasures of the World*, informs us that the literal translation has twice been published in France. You may like to try your hand at it yourself. It begins: APRE: MEY UNE PAIRE DE PIJON TIRESKET 2 COEURS QESEAJ TETE CHERALF UNE KORT FIL WINSHIENT ECU PRENEY UNE CULLIERE DEMI. . . . This is translated as: 'After (or first): a pair of pigeons draw aside 2 hearts [unidentifiable] head of horse a "kort fil winshient" shield take a spoon half. . . .'

The treasure on Mahé has not been recovered, but if I were to choose to hunt any of these caches, I would try the one in the Poudre d'Or, Mauritius.

The Concealment of the Big Horn Gold

Once the hint of a lost cache reaches the ears of the treasure hunter, his first step is to verify, as far as is possible, the true facts of the tale. Pinpointing the time and place of interment is generally the result of many hours of painstaking research into ancient historical chronicles, some of them dealing with events that are by no means obscure. Only when this research has been accomplished can any field work usefully begin.

A recent example was the discovery of information about a hitherto forgotten cache of gold connected with the Indian massacre of General Custer and his men in 1876, by the American writer, Emile C. Schurmacher. While investigating a missing shipment of gold, Schurmacher was researching an official operations report written by General Alfred H. Terry, which in turn led to the examination of long-forgotten river-boat logs. He suddenly found that his quest was leading straight to the scene of Custer's historic last stand, and timed almost to the day. In the national outcry that followed the massacre, news of the missing shipment had been pushed into the background, soon to be forgotten altogether.

Glancing through the dossier of facts compiled by Schurmacher, it is remarkable how the paths and actions of the central characters mesh unknowingly into a strange and sad sequence of events.

It was on 22 June 1876, in the area bounded by the rivers Big Horn, Little Big Horn and Little Horn, that General Custer received information regarding the position of a large force of Sioux Indians. The general quickly issued orders to the five companies of the Seventh Cavalry under his command to break camp and set out on the trail of the Indians. Custer was proud of his fighting force and extremely confident of success against the Sioux. General Terry sent word, offering extra men, but Custer declined.

Two days later at Fort Bufford, some way down the Big Horn, the river boat *Far West*, under the command of fifty-two-year-old Grant Marsh, was on hire to the US Cavalry for the purpose of delivering supplies. The boat, constructed in Pittsburgh some six years previously, had been specially designed for navigating tricky rivers comparable to the shallow, upper parts of the Missouri. 190 feet in length, with a beam of 33 feet, the *Far West* only drew twenty inches of water when empty and as little as four and a half feet when fully loaded to her 400-ton capacity. On that day the boat left Fort Bufford and plied upstream to a pre-arranged rendezvous with General Terry at the spot where the Little Big Horn River joins the Big Horn.

In the open country, sixty miles east of the Little Horn, Custer's scouts brought news of a recently deserted Indian village near the river. The general decided to make camp and rest. At 11.00 pm, he gave the order to move once more, and he and his contingent rode on through the night.

Earlier in the day, on a rough trail about fifty miles west of the Big Horn River, driver Gil Longworth and two armed guards, Dickson and Jergens, were en route from Bozeman, Montana. They were heading for Bismark, North Dakota, in a mule-drawn freight wagon carrying a shipment of miners' gold worth about £30000. The gold was in the form of nuggets and dust, packed in leather bags each bearing a label with the name of the owner.

By 25 June the *Far West*, on her slow journey upstream was approaching the rendezvous. At daybreak Custer and his men arrived at a point only fifteen miles from the Little Horn River, the spot where the Indian village had been situated. Here, they made camp.

While Custer's men were resting, Gil Longworth had driven to within a few miles of the Big Horn River, and was by now a badly worried man. Twice the wagon had been chased by hostile

Indians. He had managed to outrun them, but Longworth and the two guards were not happy about their chances of making it through to Bismark.

At mid-day Custer broke camp and rode after the Sioux, who had been seen mounting and riding hastily away. Encouraged, the general went in hot pursuit and, later in the day, engaged the Indians in an area near the Little Big Horn River. A few miles away, another commanding officer, Major Reno, was desperately fighting off a large force of Sioux. Soon after this, overpowering numbers of Indians, led by Sitting Bull, Gall and Crazy Horse, overran Custer and annihilated his 261 men.

The following day, two of General Terry's scouts arrived at the rendezvous to find that the *Far West* was not there. Assuming that the supply boat had not yet arrived, they moved downstream to meet her. But Captain Marsh had in fact previously been to the designated point, and having never navigated so far up the Big Horn, was uncertain if the river he could see was actually the Little Big Horn, or just another unnamed tributary swollen by rain. He sent some men out in a small boat, but after rowing four miles up the tributary they returned and expressed the belief that it was not the Little Big Horn. Captain Marsh had decided to move further up the Big Horn, and he was now some fifteen or twenty miles upstream. Soundings indicated that the depth had dwindled to a mere three and a half feet and, as the flat-bottomed craft was drawing three feet, he could go no further. Since it was now late in the afternoon, he dropped anchor, intending to return downstream in the morning. He now realized that the tributary he saw had in fact been the rendezvous point.

In the early evening, the crew of the *Far West* heard a shout from the shore and found that Gil Longworth with his wagon had arrived at the river. Longworth asked to come aboard for an urgent conference with Marsh. He appeared extremely agitated and tired. When he was ferried to the ship, he told Marsh that the surrounding country was swarming with hostile Indians, and begged him to take the shipment of gold on board, and to deliver it to Bismark when he could. Seeing Longworth's predicament, Captain Marsh agreed, and the sacks of gold were hurriedly transferred to the *Far West*.

Longworth and his two companions then drove off to the west, intending to return to Bozeman.

As twilight turned to dusk, Marsh's attention was caught by the sight of many columns of smoke rising from Indian camp-fires in the vicinity. It indicated an unusually large force and Marsh realized that Longworth had not underestimated the danger. He became increasingly worried and began to regret accepting the responsibility for the gold shipment. After a great deal of deliberation, he reached the conclusion that it would be safer if it were cached in some concealed place on the shore, to be collected at a later date.

Immediately, he ordered the deck-hands to put the bags into two boats and row them ashore, there to be stacked up on the river bank. The men then returned to the boat, leaving Marsh, his First Mate, Ben Thompson, and his engineer, Foulk, to hide the gold. In three and a half hours they were back on board the *Far West* with their job done.

Not very far away, Major Reno and his men had been trapped all day atop a hill surrounded by Sioux warriors. There was no way to escape and they were hoping for relief from Custer, not knowing that he had been massacred. Further down the river, a Colonel Wier was endeavouring to push through to Reno, but was repulsed.

Early in the morning of 27 June, Marsh weighed anchor and moved off downstream to return to the mouth of the Little Big Horn. There, moored on a small island in mid-river to forestall any sneak attacks, he waited for news from General Terry. Terry's two scouts, farther down the river, realized that they had missed the *Far West* and turned about to retrace their steps.

At the hills (later named Reno's Hill) Major Reno and his men were in a bad way and short of water. Suddenly they observed a panic among the Indians, who began to withdraw, and Reno saw that General Terry was attacking them from the rear. The Indians were routed, and a Lieutenant Bradley reported finding Custer and his men all dead and, as was the Indian custom, badly mutilated.

The next day the bodies of Dickson and Jergens were found at a place called Pryor's Creek. They had been killed by Indians and the wagon burned, but there was no sign of Gil Longworth.

At the rendezvous point two members of the *Far West*'s crew, out fishing on the river bank, met a Crow Indian scout called Curly. By using signs, he conveyed to them that he was the living witness to the massacre of Custer and his men. In reply to their questions, he explained how he hid in a field after the massacre, covering himself with a discarded Sioux blanket. Catching a riderless pony, he had managed to get away unnoticed.

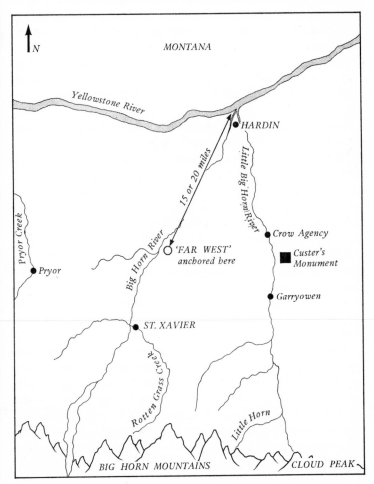

A map showing the area in which the Big Horn Treasure was lost.

Later in the afternoon, the two scouts appeared at the rendezvous and, having now located the *Far West*, departed at once to inform General Terry of the boat's arrival.

On 29 June two couriers arrived at the *Far West* and handed Marsh urgent instructions from General Terry, also relaying the news about Custer. Marsh was instructed to prepare his ship to receive and transport the many wounded soldiers down river to Bismark. He realized that there would be no time to go back and recover the gold shipment. Major Reno and his men were already convoying the injured across country to meet the *Far West*.

By 30 June the bullet-riddled body of Gil Longworth had been found at Clark's Fork. He had been dead for several days, having escaped the Indians, but being mortally wounded in the process.

The wounded soldiers reached the *Far West* and were taken on board. General Terry arrived and instructed Marsh to take them to Bismark with all possible speed. Marsh accordingly weighed anchor, and arrived at Bismark on 5 July.

With the Sioux on the warpath, Marsh made no attempt to recover the gold, and it is unlikely that either Ben Thompson or Foulk tried either. But Marsh did not forget about it. In 1879 he returned to Bozeman and attempted to trace the freight company that had employed Gil Longworth, only to find that, due to the continual attacks on their shipments by the Indians, the company had been forced out of business. Further, he was not able to trace any of the company records, in which he had expected to find the names of the original owners of the gold. Those names were on the labels clipped to the bags.

Schurmacher is convinced that the gold shipment still lies where Marsh hid it. His investigation into the river boat records revealed that Marsh continued to skipper river boats until 1906, when he retired at the age of seventy-two. He was thought of as an honest citizen, much commended for his part in the Indian campaigns. It is documented that he tried to locate the owners of the shipment and throughout the rest of his life there is no indication of sudden, unaccounted-for affluence.

In 1879, the *Far West* was sold and put to work plying

between St Louis, Missouri, and ports lower down the river. Mate Ben Thompson went with her, while Marsh took command of another packet which plied between Bismark and Yellowstone. Engineer Foulk went with him, but in 1892 retired to Sioux City in poor health. All three men remained working, a fact which is recorded in the river boat logs, and there is no record of sudden wealth being a feature in the lives of either Thompson or Foulk.

Marsh, Thompson and Foulk were the only three people who knew the exact location of the cache. Assuming that they did not recover the gold themselves, there is always the possibility that any one of them could have passed on the information to friends or relatives, but this would have provided only a little more chance of a discovery being effected than exists for a treasure hunter today. We can assume that Marsh did not mark the cache too conspicuously for fear that the Indians, who had extremely sharp eyes, would notice that the earth had been disturbed. Therefore, he would have been able only to give certain landmarks as the guide, landmarks that would no doubt be found to fit other spots along the river.

The clues we have are these. The spot is 'fifteen to twenty miles up the Big Horn River from the mouth of the Little Big Horn', on the west bank, since Longworth was coming from the west. The area containing the cache must be small, since Marsh had no horses when he was hiding the gold. It all had to be carried, so it couldn't have been taken very far if it was buried or cached in three and a half hours. The fact that the river was only three and a half feet deep at the time does not help a great deal, since the depth of the river would vary with every heavy rainfall. We do however know that it happened in June and there are no reasons to assume that 1876 was an exceptional year for rainfall.

Of course, any of the crew members, who were aware of what was happening, may have returned in an attempt to find the gold, and perhaps some tried. But they too, even though they had been at the site and would possibly recognize the spot again, would still be unaware of the actual hole where the gold was stored.

Emile Schurmacher seems convinced, from his researches,

that the cache is still there and has already made one attempt to locate it – unsuccessfully.

The nearest town to the location is called Hardin and lies on the main highway between Billings, Montana, and Sheridan, Wyoming. The monument to General Custer is just off US Highway 90.

Derrotero de Valverde

Towards the end of the sixteenth century, Juan Valverde, a Spanish volunteer for the New World, arrived in Ecuador and, after being stationed in the main town of Quito for several months, was posted to a small garrison in the village of Ambato. For a young man, it turned out to be an extremely dull, lonely job and, during the four or five years that he was there, he began courting an Indian girl of the Salasaca tribe. The remote, garrison life finally became more than Valverde could stand. One day, he and his Indian girl friend rode out of Ambato determined never to come back.

Heading east, they made their way to the remote mountain village of Pillaro, the home of the girl's parents. Here the couple were married and together they settled down among the Indians, who accepted Valverde as one of the tribe. Pillaro was set in a remote part of these high mountains and it seemed unlikely that he – a deserter – would ever be traced, but one day a patrol of Spanish soldiers entered the village and made camp. Valverde and the Indians watched anxiously as a defensive post was established at the south end of the *pueblo*. It looked as if the soldiers intended to remain.

Fortunately, Valverde was not recognized by the newcomers but he realized it would be only a matter of time and so he decided to make his way back to Spain. There was, however, one problem. He had not enough money to take his wife with him. So the Indians held a hurried conference and decided to fund Valverde from a secret hoard of tribal wealth, artifacts of gold which had been stripped from the temples and buried after the savage murder of their Inca king, Atahualpa.

69

Taking eight burros, they set out on the three-week trek to the site of the hidden treasure and returned with an enormous quantity of solid gold artifacts. Valverde, now fully accepted by the tribe, was allowed to go with them and thus learnt the route to the secret hiding place. On their return to Pillaro, the gold was crudely melted down into bars and then carried by mule over the mountains and down into the port of Guayaquil. To prevent the treasure being impounded, Valverde confided in a close friend of his army days, Padre Olmedo Alvarado. The priest agreed to put the seal of the church on the shipment and so make it inviolate to army confiscation.

Valverde arrived back in Spain, sold the gold and overnight became a wealthy man. His sudden affluence did not go unnoticed and although he tried to suppress the rumours, news of his riches eventually reached the ears of King Philip II of Spain. Valverde was summoned to the court and an explanation was demanded. Piece by piece, the story was extracted from him, and on threat of imprisonment or death for his desertion, he was forced to write down detailed instructions for locating the rest of the hidden hoard. A copy of this *Derrotero*, as it was called, was sent to the Corregidors of Tacunga and Ambato, with a commission to mount an expedition to find the treasure.

Headed by the Corregidor of Tacunga in person, and accompanied by Padre Longo, a friar with a considerable literary reputation, the expedition set out, following the instructions in the *Derrotero*. Any doubts as to the authenticity of the document were soon dispelled, for it was found that the details within corresponded so closely to the topography that only someone who had actually experienced the journey could have drawn it up.

The expedition had almost reached the end of the route when, one evening, Padre Longo disappeared, and no trace of him could be found. To this day, exactly what befell the unlucky friar is uncertain, but it is probable that he either fell into a ravine or got trapped in one of the many morasses which surrounded their campsite. After searching in vain for some days, the Corregidor finally gave orders to return to Tacunga. The expedition was thus thwarted.

In the years immediately following, the story of Valverde's *Derrotero* began to circulate and many adventurers visited the archives at Tacunga to copy the famous manuscript. Yet there is no record of anyone ever reaching or reclaiming the hidden treasure of the Salasacas. Just why this should be, is hard to say, for the directions laid down by the Spanish deserter are clear and comprehensive.

'Once you have reached the village of Pillaro,' the *Derrotero* begins, 'ask for the Hacienda La Moya and sleep the first night a little beyond it. Here, the Indians will point out Mount Guapa, which summit will be discernible if the day is clear.' At this point Valverde was given one of the most important clues to the location of the treasure. He was instructed to stand with his back to Ambato and look eastwards, where he would be able to see the triple peak of Llanganati Mountain. On the slopes of this most unusual landmark was located an artificial lake, into which the Indians had thrown vast quantities of gold that was to have been Atahualpa's ransom.

The *Derrotero* continues:

This then, is your final destination. Although to reach it is a most difficult and arduous journey.

Reaching Mount Guapa, proceed through a deep wood called 'La Floresta' until you reach a wide, swampy terrain and after crossing it, turn to the left and follow a small pathway which the Indians used in bringing the gold to the burial site. Following in this direction, you will eventually come upon two small lakes called *anteojoes*, or 'eye-glasses', because in the centre there is a slight projection of land which resembles a nose.

From this point you will again see the Llanganati Mountain which you first saw from the top of Mount Guapa. I advise you to leave these lakes towards the left, swinging round until you come to the projection of earth resembling the nose. Ahead of you, you will see a broad valley which is where you can make camp.

There you must leave your horses and continue by foot in the same direction until you arrive at a large, black lake called Yana-Cocha and you must follow the shore-line of this lake along the left-hand side. From this point on, the terrain becomes exceedingly rough and you must descend the cordillera in such a way that you will arrive at a canyon in which there is a large waterfall. There you will find a bridge consisting of three tree-trunks.

The Corregidor of Tacunga and his party followed these

directions, crossed the tree-trunk bridge and then followed the trail through the forest until they arrived at a large cave. Here they spent the third night of their expedition.

The next morning they continued according to the manuscript's instructions which read: 'Follow the trail in the same direction until you come to a canyon, which is very deep and dry.' This they bridged as best they could. On the fourth night, they rested at an Indian camping ground, which, as the manuscript told them, was easily recognizable by the number of old clay pots scattered around. Marching steadily, the next day took them to a small mountain which, as Valverde had noted, was entirely covered in daisies. To the left of this, he added, there was a little valley in which grew a certain type of straw from which the Indians wove their hats and shoes.

The party then continued to a waterfall, which actually descended from the arm of the Llanganati Hills and which was situated on the right-hand side of the trail. In the stream at the bottom of the fall, Valverde mentions, there were great quantities of gold nuggets. But they were not yet at their destination.

The manuscript continues: 'To climb the hill directly in front of you, you must cross the brook and veer to the right, eventually passing the top of the waterfall and circling a small arm of the mountain.' On their left, they noticed an ancient Indian smelter for refining gold and, upon examination, saw that the oven was actually constructed with solid gold nails.

Ahead of you is a third range of mountains which you must reach, for here, in the foothills is the lake which bears the golden treasure of the ancient Indians. If you get lost while travelling through the woods, look for the river and follow it along its banks to the right. Further on, you will find a canyon which is impossible to cross, but by proceeding further along the river bank, you will eventually be able to scale the mountain on its right flank. Once this has been done, the artificial lake will be found in a small, beautiful valley and in the water you will locate the golden treasure I have described.

In possession of such a precise list of directions, one wonders why the Spanish expedition failed in its mission; or indeed whether it really did fail. Was the treasure discovered and the fact kept secret? It is possible but unlikely, because there were so many people taking part that news of that kind would have leaked out. The reputed proportions of the hoard could scarcely guarantee a continuing silence. And what about Valverde? The *Derrotero* had been found to be accurate, right up until the last few miles, but it was written under duress. Would he have dared to mislead by laying a false end to a genuine trail? In view of the terrors of a Spanish torture chamber, it seems unlikely that he would be so reckless.

In the 1850s a British botanist, Richard Spruce, spent several years investigating the authenticity of the *Derrotero*. He eventually found what he described as indisputable proof that the document had been originally sent from Spain, and the subsequent expedition had taken place as described. In an article written for the journal of the Royal Geographical Society in 1861, he stated that the *Cedula Real* (the royal commission for the expedition) and the *Derrotero* had been deposited in the archives of Tacunga, but that they had disappeared from there in 1840. So many people, said Spruce, were allowed in to copy the documents that, in the end, someone actually purloined the originals. He was, however, able to get hold of a copy of the *Derrotero*, dated 14 August 1827, but he was never able to determine the date of the original.

He goes on to tell of another botanist, Don Atanasio Guzman, who lived for some time in the village of Pillaro, and who made many expeditions in search of the treasure. Although he never found it, Guzman and some companions did stumble upon some ancient silver and copper mines which they worked for a while. However, it turned out to be slow and heavy labour and the novelty soon wore off. Guzman died in 1808, but he left a detailed map of the Llanganati area, which Spruce eventually traced and copied, sending the copy to the Royal Geographical Society.

In the space of three hundred and seventy years the topography of the area has been considerably altered. Courses of rivers have been changed, and violent earthquakes have rearranged the features of the terrain until it has become impossible to follow the *Derrotero* to its conclusion. The many who have tried have stated that they have been able to follow Valverde's trail for several days, but after that, the landmarks become indistinct.

In 1939 the explorer Richard D'Orsay discovered a 19 000-foot peak with a triangular shape. It is now known as Cerro Hermosa. On each side there stood a similar triangular peak, and D'Orsay found that these three peaks could be seen in the far distance from Pillaro – providing the weather allowed – just as Valverde stated. D'Orsay was convinced that the lake was somewhere on the side of Cerro Hermosa, but over the years gigantic landslides have covered it with tons of rock, changing the entire face of the mountain.

No expedition can be easy. From Pillaro there are no trails and horses can only be used for one day's march. After that, you must travel on foot, carrying your supplies on your back, crossing tremendous gorges and inching across log bridges. To reach Cerro Hermosa it is necessary to walk for miles through marshland covered with razor-sharp sawgrass. Near-vertical cliffs often have to be scaled. Eleven months of the year a cold icy rain falls, rivers flood and knee-deep bogs are commonplace. Food is extremely scarce and experts have called it the most inhospitable terrain in the world. Even helicopters, which were recently tried, were forced to give up because of bad visibility. Any treasure hunt in this wild region must be confined to the short – and unreliable – period of fine weather in the summer.

In 1949 a devastating earthquake struck the Pillaro area with a strange result. Walking across a great plateau near the village, an Indian discovered a beautiful golden urn which had been thrown to the surface by the upheaval. Subsequent investigation revealed that the plateau was a pre-Inca burial site with an estimated forty thousand graves. Since the plateau lay at an elevation of 15 000 feet and was constantly swept by chilling winds, few seekers arrived at first. In the early sixties, however, New York's *Argosy* magazine published an article about the plateau. Almost immediately, swarms of treasure hunters appeared and the small village underwent a minor boom. Government decree finally closed the site to all but authorized archaeologists.

In recent years the situation has remained unchanged, but it is generally conceded that Swiss explorer and treasure hunter Eugene Brunner has the best chance of locating the long-lost Valverde treasure. He has trekked into the mountains for over twenty years and has succeeded in photographing a few of the original landmarks mentioned in the *Derrotero*. He now has a permanent camp at the base of Cerro Hermosa to which he returns each year to dig.

Seldom is such a document backed by a weight of expert opinion in favour of its authenticity. There are corroborating documents in the Archivos Indios in La Rabida, Spain, as well as papers proving the existence of Valverde in the Biblioteca Nacional, Madrid. These days Ambato is a major town and both it and the village of Pillaro lie close to the Pan-American highway. The three peaks of Llanganati Mountain (Cerro Hermosa) lie to the east.

A Hoard in Huachuca Canyon

The hoard in Huachuca Canyon is the story of a lost fortune in gold and silver ingots. It is really two tales in one but both accounts are well authenticated and there is little doubt about their connection.

In 1879 four Arizona bandits rode into the Davis Mountains in Jeff Davis County, Texas. Their leader was 'Red Curley' (Andrew King), and his henchmen were Zwing Hunt, Jim Hughes, and John ('Doc') Neal. For several years, this quartet had made a profitable living from their frequent raids into Mexico and were on their way to rendezvous with a Mexican outlaw named Juan Estrada and his gang. A meeting took place, at which it was planned that the two groups should join forces in order to raid the mint at Monterrey, Mexico.

The first stage in the plan was to obtain transport and to this end they camped near an army outpost called Fort Davis. Here they waited for a moment when they could catch the troops off guard, and stole some mules that were grazing near the fort. Taking about sixty of the animals, they drove them south across the Mexican border, eventually arriving at the small town of Presidio. There Juan Estrada and his men joined up with the four from Arizona. Twenty-six strong, the gang started southward with their long string of mules. Two days from Presidio, they stopped at some bat caves and filled a supply of sacks with bat guano, so as to appear as a group of respectable traders bringing fertilizer to sell at the market in Monterrey.

Monterrey is a rich cathedral town, the capital of the province of Nuervo Leon, with the mint and gold smelter located in the centre. No federal troops were stationed in the town, the guarding of the mint being the duty of the local *rurales*. Red Curley and the outlaws moved into town and took up their position at the market where they sold the fertilizer. On the evening before the raid took place, members of the gang had managed to strike up an acquaintance with many of the *rurales*, and they now invited them to wine and dine on the proceeds of their marketing endeavours.

At midnight, while most of the guards were drunk, the bandits raided the mint and blasted the vault where the ingots were stored. Quickly, the treasure was loaded onto the waiting mules and driven out of town. It is estimated that each of the twenty-eight mules that left Monterrey carried 150 pounds of treasure. Remaining mules of the original pack or *remuda* travelled unburdened so that they could take over the load on the following day, thus allowing the gang to make a fast time on their return trip to Texas.

Having crossed the border, the group made their way north-west into the Davis Mountains. Red Curley had already selected a cave near El Muerto Spring as a suitable hiding place for the loot and, some twenty miles or so before they reached the cave, he told Estrada that he and his men would ride ahead and scout the country. But Estrada should never have trusted Curley. To reach the cave the mule-train had to traverse a narrow canyon; as the mules were herded through, Estrada and his men were gunned down by crossfire from Red Curley's gang. The ambush was completely successful and Red Curley rounded up the mule-train and continued the journey.

It has always been thought that Red Curley and his gang took the loot to the cave at El Muerto Spring and hid it there, blocking the entrance to the cave before they left. However, it was never conclusively proved for the simple reason that the stolen hoard was never found. Records show that the infamous four returned to their stamping ground in Arizona, for 'Doc' Neal is reported to have been killed by a sheriff's posse, Zwing Hunt was captured and jailed in Tombstone and Red Curley was caught in Shakespeare, New Mexico, where he was reputedly hanged from the rafters of the Pioneer House dining room. Only Jim Hughes escaped a violent end and, for a while, ran a saloon in Lordsburg.

Discoveries made in later years seem to indicate that the gang actually took the loot all the way back to Arizona, where they cached it in an underground vault situated in a lonely canyon only thirty miles from their favourite haunt, the town of Tombstone.

There was a lapse of over sixty years before the next episode of this story took place. In 1941 Private Robert Jones, a thirty-seven-year-old Negro soldier from Texas, was stationed at Fort Huachuca, in southern Arizona, where he worked during the week with a post construction group. The camp was in a rather remote area and devoid of any of the usual big city attractions. Tombstone, only twenty-two miles away, was of some historic significance, but by then pretty well deserted. Other towns were even farther away, and lack of entertainment made weekends periods of frustration. Some of the men spent their free time exploring the surrounding countryside, but this held little attraction for Jones. The camp embraced roughly 73 500 acres, most of which was wasteland – hardly an area suitable for a weekend stroll.

One Sunday, however, out of sheer boredom Jones and his friend Sam Mays decided to go out on an exploratory trip. They headed for the hills which jutted up out of the flat terrain, several miles from their barracks, and climbed up into a place known as Huachuca Canyon. With Jones leading, the two men traversed the floor of the canyon for about two miles. Suddenly there was a crashing sound and Mays looked round to find that Jones had disappeared. Mays quickly saw that the ground had given way under his friend's weight, and that he had fallen into a concealed shaft.

Jones landed with a crash that jarred him, but he was unhurt. When he got to his feet, he saw that he had slipped down a narrow shaft resembling an old well hole. As his eyes grew accustomed to the gloom, he perceived a tunnel cut into one side of the shaft. Reassuring Mays, who was peering down from the rim of the hole, he felt his way into the tunnel, and found that he was in the entrance to another room. In the pitch blackness, he ran exploratory fingers round the walls and made an amazing discovery. The sides of the room were lined with metal ingots, stacked against the wall.

Meanwhile, Mays had procured a length of vine with which to get Jones out. Discussing their find, the two men returned to camp and procured a flashlight and a tape measure. Mays also took a length of rope and, back at the hole, they secured it to a nearby tree and Jones lowered himself into the pit once more. With the aid of his steel tape, Jones ascertained that the room at the bottom of the shaft was six feet square. The tunnel leading off from it was five feet long, leading into a room fifteen feet by twenty feet, with a ceiling height of six feet. The rooms appeared to be natural underground caverns although the corners had been squared by hand.

There were two stacks of metal bars against the wall of the inner room. Jones measured some of the ingots, finding that they were sixteen by four by two inches and weighing, as far as he was able to judge, about sixty pounds each. Some of the bars were grey, almost black in colour, while those in the other stack were yellow. Each stack was twenty feet long, four feet high and eight inches wide.

Jones left the bars exactly as he found them, but when he returned to camp he reported the find to his sergeant. The sergeant had been a sceptical listener to many a story of buried gold, none of which had turned out to be true, and he advised Jones to forget the whole thing.

The following weekend saw the two men back at the shaft. Once more Jones descended into the room, but this time he had brought a hatchet with him. He used it to hack a piece off one of the gold bars, the steel of the blade easily cutting into the soft, heavy metal of the ingot. At the first opportunity, he acquired a three-day pass and went to the town of Douglas, some sixty miles distant, and the smelting centre for the rich ore that was brought out from nearby Mule Mountain. He sought the local assayer and gave him the sample. Taking the piece of ingot, the assayer disappeared for an hour and a half. Just when Jones was beginning to feel uneasy, he returned and gave the soldier eight hundred dollars in bills. But when he began to question the source of the gold Jones became frightened and left. The proceeds of the sale he spent on a big party for his platoon.

It seems incredible that, after this, the soldier did absolutely nothing about his find. Perhaps he was afraid. For a year he kept away from the cache, but one Sunday he slipped out of camp and revisited the site of the shaft, having decided to camouflage the entrance to the underground room. He wedged a large boulder in the shaft entrance and then shovelled dirt on top until the shaft could no longer be distinguished. To mark the spot so that he could find it again, he carved the letters 'J.R.' on a rock close by.

Jones was physically unsuitable for active service and so, in February of 1944 when his unit was sent to the Pacific, he remained behind at Camp Huachuca. Sam Mays had been transferred to another unit in 1942, and later was sent to Italy where he was killed in action. After the war, Jones returned to Texas without ever having revisited the vault. Fort Huachuca was closed in 1947 and used as a wildlife sanctuary, although it was reopened in 1950 and, four years later, turned into an electrical proving ground.

For fourteen years Jones kept the secret of the hidden treasure vault to himself, but in 1959 he decided that he would attempt to recover some of the ingots from it. He returned to Fort Huachuca and poured out the whole story to the commanding officer, Colonel Elbridge Bacon, who gave him permission to go out into the hills and dig.

Accompanied by a security guard, Jones went up into the canyon until he spied his carved rock marker. Over the years, rainfall had caused the surface of the filled-in shaft to sink a little below the level of the ground, and so it was easy enough to find. They began to dig. Towards the end of the day, the colonel came out to see how they were getting on but although the men had been at work since the morning, the rock ground had only yielded a hole a few feet deep. The colonel offered to help, and the next morning he sent up an army bulldozer, which began boring at the spot indicated by Jones.

By noon, there was a huge hole in the ground almost fifty feet wide and a dozen feet deep. Later that day, Colonel Bacon arrived to find a hole big enough to hold a house but nothing had been discovered and the hole was beginning to fill with water. Disappointed that the bulldozer had failed to uncover anything, he had no choice but to order that the hole be filled in again. Jones returned to Texas and the men at Fort Huachuca dismissed his story as another 'buried gold' fable.

Several months later, Colonel Bacon received a letter containing two sworn affidavits from two men who had been at the Fort with Jones in 1941. The statements told how Jones had found a chunk of gold and what he had told them of its origin. It also described the party that Jones had thrown on the proceeds of what the assayer had given him for the sample. When Jones arrived at the Fort again, Colonel Bacon asked him why he had not mentioned cutting off a piece of the gold and selling it, to which Jones replied that he had been afraid.

Armed with Jones' description of the assayer, the colonel drove to Douglas to see if he could check the story. He found a man who seemed to fit perfectly the description given by Jones, but the man denied all knowledge of buying a chunk of gold from a soldier. That seemed to settle the matter, but something kept nagging at the colonel. How had Jones been able to give such an accurate description of the man? It was only some time later that he realized the man had been lying when he denied all knowledge of Jones and his piece of gold – he was afraid of the penalties of the Gold Reserve Act, which could have meant imprisonment.

The colonel decided to make another attempt to locate the underground vault, and hired a rig using a drill that weighed 1800 pounds, with which he cut a hole six inches in diameter. When the giant drill reached the sixteen-foot level, it broke through into an empty space. Six feet of the drill protruded into a cavity. The drill was removed and a derrick with a clamshell scoop was put in its place. The operator got down to twelve feet before he was forced to stop because water was pouring into the hole at the rate of fifty gallons a minute. Ordered to keep going the operator dug the scoop down to the thirty-two-foot level, and then struck solid rock.

The next day, a rock drill was brought in and five holes were drilled in the rock bed. Six sticks of dynamite were placed in each hole and at 1.30 in the afternoon the blast went off.

Practically nothing was accomplished by the explosion, except that the hole was made into a bigger mess than ever before, and the army finally decided to call it a day.

Jones again returned to Texas and the story of the treasure hunt was gradually forgotten.

Three years later, on 21 October 1962, the *Dallas Morning News* printed a small announcement which said that Robert Jones of Dallas had received permission from the Department of the Army to resume his search. Unfortunately Jones was by now too ill to come and head the renewed search, so arrangements were made with a Prescott building contractor to supply and operate the necessary heavy earth-moving equipment. The contractor himself had agreed to finance the venture in return for a share of the proceeds of the treasure. When his total commitment reached 8000 dollars without any sign of the stacks of ingots being found, he was forced to quit.

Jones died in 1969 and it seems that all efforts to locate the missing hoard ceased. He wrongly estimated the weight of the bars, since a bar of gold of the size he stipulated would weigh 89 pounds. A bar of silver of the same dimensions weighs about 49 pounds. His measured description of the cache would place its value, at today's prices, somewhere in the region of twelve million pounds.

As to whether the cache really is the hoard hidden by Red Curley is open to discussion. Although the Monterrey robbery did take place as described, the connection with the vault in Huachuca Canyon is unproved and may be a gimmick thought up by the army publicity department in the absence of a better explanation.

According to the statements made by Jones, he wedged a large boulder into the mouth the tunnel just below the opening, and then shovelled dirt on top until he had filled it to ground level, after which he placed his marker. It seems inconceivable that anyone would leave a find like that lying there for fourteen years, but he did just that. Was he so sure that, on his return after so long, the marker was in the right place, or that he was digging in the right place?

Although he stated that he easily found the spot where the filled-in shaft lay because of the depression in the ground, it would be difficult to be so confident after that length of time, and the results seem to indicate that he had not been right. It depends entirely on whether the stone marker was small enough to have been moved, either by flood waters or by human hand.

If he was digging in the right spot, the use of the heavy machinery, and finally dynamite, set the seal on the mission's failure. The presence of water was unfortunate and over the years an earth tremor may have changed the course of an underground stream. The name 'Huachuca' is an old Apache word meaning 'mountains with water'.

According to Jones' story, the cache is not deep, but it will have to be unearthed in the same way as it was buried – by hand. Should it be found, though, according to the US laws of treasure trove, the government would take 60 per cent and the rest would be taxable.

Hidden Hoards of the Jesuits

Many treasure legends have been connected with activities of the Society of Jesus – better known as the Jesuits. This militant religious Order was founded in Spain in 1534, by a knight named Ignatius Loyola, and it was soon so well established that in 1543 it gained recognition from the Pope. In a short time, the Order grew to become an international power, not only in religious matters, but inevitably in politics as well. The members became a substantial force in the Counter-Reformation.

The rapid growth of Jesuit power certainly worried Philip II of Spain, and in 1592 he passed a law to limit their control of the country's wealth. Undeterred, Loyola's followers sent missionaries to Mexico, Brazil, Peru and Bolivia, where the Fathers were not slow to take advantage of the abundant mineral wealth that was to be had for the taking. In these new colonies they established many hundreds of mines and at each mine, or area of mines, they built a mission from which they tried to convert the savage Indians, simultaneously exploiting them as a labour force to work underground.

News of the rich yields of silver and gold which the industrious padres were extracting from the bowels of 'New Spain' soon reached the ears of the Old World king and he hurriedly implemented a decree that would ensure the Crown a share of the wealth. The new law demanded that the Jesuits surrender 20 per cent of their mineral takings to the treasury of Spain. This levy became known as the Royal Fifth.

Not unnaturally, the Fathers were reluctant to comply with this demand, but many of them sent token 'fifths' in order to pacify the court. But it soon became apparent to the Spanish Treasury that the crafty Fathers were cooking the books. In fact, many of the missions refused to contribute at all and, as the relations between the Order and the Crown slowly deteriorated, the Jesuits complied with the decree less and less. Instead, they began to stockpile ingots of gold and silver, waiting to see what would develop.

In 1767 the Order was expelled from South America. For some time shipments of bullion had been suspended so that the Fathers could amass enough to buy a portion of land in Bolivia to turn into a Jesuit colony independent of Spain. This plan failed, and aware of their impending expulsion, many of the priests sealed the caves and hiding places they had so carefully constructed, and left the country, hoping no doubt to return at a later date.

This happened too in Mexico, where again the Jesuits were in control of some of the richest mines in the country. But in 1767 the axe fell and the Jesuits were expelled from Spain, France and Portugal, and in 1773 the Order was suppressed.

While they flourished the Jesuits had established themselves over a wide area of the New World in places as far apart as Colorado and Chile. Accounts of their mines gave rise to many stories of hidden treasure and countless expeditions have been mounted to try to unearth their stockpiles of silver and gold, as well as the many valuable religious artifacts that were buried in the same caches.

One of the best substantiated of these stories is the tale that began in 1736, when Spanish explorers discovered one of the richest silver veins ever to be found in North America. Located just south of the Cerro Ruido Mountains in the Pajarito Range (nowadays known as the Oro Blanco Mountains), the mine was named La Purisima Concepción, a title which clearly indicated clerical influence. It was reputedly operating as late as 1750, when the Pima Indians staged their second uprising and drove all soldiers and priests from the region, burning and plundering the missions. But the revolt subsided, and the mine was reopened about four years later.

No doubt ancient Spanish or Mexican documents have some reference to the Concepción mine, but the only recent information was found by a ranch owner who, while searching through ancient papers at the Tumacacori mission, came upon an old *derrotero* describing the location of the mine.

About three leagues from the mines of Nuestra Señora de Guadalupe, in a southerly direction, there is a pass called 'Pass of Janos'. From this pass emerges a rivulet which empties into the Santa Cruz River. The mine is to the left of the pass. Below the pass there are two *patios* [open spaces] and 12 *arrastres* [ore-crushers]. The mine was a tunnel 300 *varas* in length [275 yards]. This tunnel had the name of LA PURISIMA CONCEPCION carved out with a chisel. The tunnel runs in a northerly direction, 100 *varas* in length [about 91 yards]. The ore is yellow and runs half silver and one-fifth gold.

In a northerly direction, 50 *varas* [about 45 yards] from the mouth of the mine, there are some ash pits. Here, virgin silver was found that ranged in weight from one pound to five *arrobas* [125 pounds]. The mine was closed with a copper door which had enormous hinges and a hasp.

The first Tumacacori mission was built on the west bank of the river, about three miles to the south and half a mile west of the site of the present one which is now a national monument and protected. The latter can be found on the east bank of the Rio Santa Cruz, about forty-eight miles south of Tucson, Arizona, on Highway 89. One can see from the document that finding the Concepción mine depends to a large extent on pinpointing the location of the Guadalupe mine. According to old documents, the Guadalupe mine was supposed to be one league south, or south-west, of the old mission. And La Purisima Concepción was placed, according to the document, three more leagues 'in a southerly direction' from the Guadalupe.

The position of the Guadalupe has never been definitely established; 'Guadalupe' was unfortunately so common a name for mines that they exist all over the south-west. Also, there remains some controversy over what constituted a 'league' in those days. The original Spanish league was long, being the equivalent of 4·214 statute miles, but it is generally thought that the New World Spanish used a league of either 3·45 miles or possibly even 2·5 miles.

Shortly after the First World War, an incident took place which may provide some indication of where the Concepción mine lay. Two army veterans, whose names have been kept secret, were prospecting in the region of Cerro Ruido (Noisy Mountain). This peak, which is one of the highest in the Pajarito (Little Bird) Range, rises to some 6000 feet. At times it emits strange sounds said to resemble the low mutter of distant thunder, or the sound of empty wagons on rock, and Indian legends, handed down orally, tell of a mine and a mission hidden within the mountain's rocky canyons.

One of the men planned to go into the town of Tucson for a week or so, but the other decided to stay on the mountain until his partner returned so, after setting a time and place for reunion, they parted company. At the appointed time, they met as planned and the man who had remained in the area reported that he had found a place where a large amount of dirt and rock at the bottom of a ledge had aroused his curiosity, since it appeared to be the results of some ancient man-made workings. After discussion, the two men agreed to investigate but on arrival at the spot, they found that they were running short of provisions. Again they decided to separate. One stayed to work at removing the earth and rocks, while the other made the short trip into Nogales for supplies.

When the partner returned from Nogales, he found his companion sleeping at the base of a tree. His clothing was torn; his face and arms were lacerated and he had a strange tale to tell.

Left on his own he had worked steadily all day at the base of the ledge until he had uncovered a small opening leading into the solid rock. On the following morning he had enlarged the hole until he was able to force an entry. Finding that he was in a dark and dusty tunnel, he used his carbide lamp to traverse the tunnel until he stumbled against a pile of shapeless sacks heaped alongside one wall. He broke open one of the sacks and found that it contained crude silver ore. There was, he estimated, about thirty tons in the pile.

He judged the tunnel to be about 400 feet long, with several branch tunnels leading off at both sides. Because nothing more could be done, he decided to postpone further exploration of the shaft until his partner returned, and to spend the time exploring the rest of the canyon.

The next day he trekked up the gully and climbed its wall, crossing over into the next canyon. Again he followed the floor upward until he eventually came upon a small opening covered with shrubs and dried, yellow grass. Through the surrounding trees he perceived the crumbling remains of an ancient church. Its walls were broken, but it was clear in outline although, since the roof had crumbled, mesquite had overgrown the unprotected interior. He realized that he had found an old mission with which the mine must be connected. He took some photographs and then, because night was approaching, made camp.

He settled down and prepared to sleep, but unaccountably was seized with an overpowering feeling of impending danger so strong that he was rigid with fear. Suddenly the silence was pierced by a blood-curdling scream. Panicking, he leapt up and plunged headlong down the canyon away from the mission, tearing through the thorny undergrowth and cannoning into boulders in the dark. Upon reaching the campsite at the mine, he collapsed, exhausted and shaken, and it was here that his partner found him on his return from Nogales.

When his friend heard this strange story, he was inclined to shrug it off as a nightmare, but the man was insistent and indicated his camera, which he had been able to salvage in his hurried flight. When developed, the films would prove the existence of the ruined mission.

However, the fortune in silver ore which lay close at hand took precedence over the mysterious mission, and they discussed the best course of action. They came to the conclusion that a sample of the ore should be taken to Tucson for an assay. Having surveyed the mine they found that it was still rich in unmined ore, so the man who had suffered the nightmare experience again elected to stay in the mountains while his companion journeyed back to Tucson. Before his partner left, he gave him the camera, telling him that there was still one frame of the film left unexposed. He could disregard this and have the roll of film developed while he was in town and thus prove that the existence of the mission was no bad dream.

The partner headed away down the trail to Nogales but when he was quite some distance from the mountain, he looked back to see that a storm was centred over the Cerro Ruido. The clouds over the peak were unusually heavy and black, presenting an awesome picture. He unstrapped the camera from his pack and used the one remaining frame on the roll to snap a picture of the storm.

At Tucson he was told that a violent storm had swept the entire region, and several minor floods had resulted. In grave concern for his friend, he completed the assay and picked up the developed snapshots without even looking at them. With as much haste as possible, he returned to the mountain, where he was alarmed to see the marks of the storm on all sides. Trees were uprooted, paths were blocked by landslides and new gullies were cut across the existing trail. At the camp, there was no sign of his friend, but as the camp was not washed out, he assumed that he might well be on another exploratory trip. Making up his sleeping bag, he settled down to wait. Two days passed with no sign of the missing man. Then the remaining partner became alarmed and went into Nogales for horses and help, but although the slopes and canyons of the Cerro Ruido were scoured for weeks, despite frequent storms, the search was fruitless.

The surviving prospector had completely overlooked the pictures that had been developed in Tucson and he now examined them. There on film were the ruins of an old mission, half-covered with wild, twisting mesquite. Another picture showed the entrance to a tunnel piercing a solid rock wall. And on the last frame was the shot that he had taken on the trail, showing the storm over the faint outline of Cerro Ruido. But, despite all searches, his partner was never found, nor have the mission or the mine ever been located again.

A lot of facts substantiate this story and the survivor appeared on a television programme in America in 1958 to give his evidence, but he insisted that his identity remain secret. All the landmarks are well known and the area is wide open to anyone who wants to go and have a look for the mission and what may have been La Purisima Concepción.

In the history of the Americas, records of the prodigious amounts of gold found in ancient Peru tend to overshadow the mineral wealth of other areas, one of the more famous of which is the Sierra Madre Mountains in Mexico. Without the documentation in Spanish and Mexican archives, the story of mining in this wild region might well be considered to be within the realm of fantasy. It has been estimated that one-third of the existing silver in the world has come from the Sierra Madre Mountains, which lie on the latitude of the 30th parallel, roughly spread over the border between northern Sonora and Chihuahua. Even today, they are considered to be one of the most rugged and awesome ranges on the North American continent.

As the Spanish *conquistadores* moved into Mexico, they executed a remorseless and greedy search for gold and silver, and inevitably with them came the Jesuit priests. In 1600 a fugitive miner discovered a rich lode of silver ore at Parral, Chihuahua, which was soon exploited by the Spanish. A hundred years later, a bandit's camp-fire revealed another rich outcropping that developed into the famed Santa Eulalia mines, a strike which by 1844 had yielded 360 million dollars and had spawned Chihuahua City. In Sonora another mine, the El Carmen, yielded lumps of pure silver weighing from 425 to 2700 pounds. About 30 million dollars' worth of the ore was taken out in the twenty years between 1730 and 1750.

During this period the Jesuits had gained control of a number of mines, one of which was the Tayopa. This mine, or rather group of mines, was discovered in 1632 and soon developed into a settlement complete with a mission church. Throughout the story of Tayopa, two other settlements are closely connected; the nearby early Spanish settlement of Guaynopa, and the Nacori mine district, which was developed in 1645.

The history of the Tayopa has been shrouded in secrecy and for a good reason. The Jesuit Fathers had formulated their own plans for the wealth that was being extracted from the mountains and these did not include payment of the Royal Fifth. Instead, they used the metal to cast religious chalices, candlesticks, crosses, tableware, and even bells, which they

90

made out of solid gold and silver. They worked the mine for a period of fourteen years and then disaster struck. In 1646 a vicious raid by the Apaches, who infested the wilder areas of the mountains, wiped out the entire settlement. When all but a handful of the men were attending a fiesta, the Indians struck, killing everyone in camp and sealing the entrance to the main mine. The last surviving document, written just prior to the massacre, is an inventory (quoted at the end of this chapter) of a large cache of treasure hidden in a vault under the church.

Thus the Tayopa was abandoned for fear of the savagery of the Indian raids, and, as the years passed, the settlement crumbled into ruins, soon to be overgrown by the surrounding jungle. In 1822 all Spanish priests were driven out of Mexico, so the documents which they possessed relating to the Tayopa and its whereabouts either lay mouldering and forgotten, or were destroyed. But the name of Tayopa was not dismissed entirely: vague hints and memories were handed down in succeeding years by word of mouth and the legend grew. A vital part of the tradition has always been to extol the virtue of the bells of the Tayopa mission, which were said to have been cast from precious metal, and were unusually sweet in tone. Is this just fantasy? Maybe, but in about 1880 one such bell was found along the border near Sahuaripa. It was cast of gold and silver and on it was inscribed: TAYOPA, GUAYNOPA, GUAYNO-PITA, SONORA. TRES MINERALES DEL MUNDO – i.e. the three richest mines in the world.

The day of the Apache – always a thorn in the side of the Spanish – was gradually drawing to a close. In 1835 the authorities resorted to human bounties, instituted by a *Proyecto de Guerra*, which placed a price on the scalp of each Apache. The result was inevitably a thinning of the existing tribes, and, fifty years later, the legendary warrior chief Geronimo was chased from the Arizona mountains down into the Sierra Madre, with US troops hard on his heels.

With the subjugation of the Indians, some of the older mines were reopened, incidentally revealing some of the barbaric cruelties practised by the Spaniards some two hundred years before. In the summer of 1881, for example, an old

Spanish mine in Hidalgo was opened up. It was found to contain the skeletons of 200 slaves, chained together, who, in desperation to see the light of day, had set the wooden framework of the mine on fire and perished to a man.

In 1896 two American prospectors rediscovered the ancient mines of Guaynopa and Guaynopita, which led to increased speculation regarding the legendary Tayopa, but the elusive mine was not to be found.

Eight years later, in 1904, Henry O. Flipper, a special agent for the US Department of Justice, was in the Sonora town of Hermosillo making survey maps of the district. Flipper, the first Negro to graduate from West Point, was an authority on Spanish law and spent much of his time in Mexico engaged in surveying and mining. At one time he was even commissioned to write a history of mining in Mexico, by the President, Porfirio Diaz.

One day, a man came to the office of the Prefect of the District of Arizpe and handed a bulky document to an assistant of General Oliveres, for whom Flipper was working. The man, Francisco Prociado, asked for officials to examine it and to suggest what assistance they could give in hunting for the mine which was named in the document – the Tayopa. It was left in the office for all to read. In appearance it was some three-quarters of an inch thick, written on foolscap paper. It was signed by three priests. General Oliveres had it sent to Mexico City for examination, where it was pronounced to be authentic. Flipper disclosed that, according to this document, all the bullion accumulated at the Tayopa had been stored until the moment of the Indian uprising. Santa Cruz, the assistant and lawyer to General Oliveres, sent out a number of expeditions to look for the mine, but all of them were fruitless.

Some time previously, Flipper had been working in the Rio Bavispe country in eastern Sonora, where he had heard of the Tayopa mine for the first time. In one of the small villages there, he saw in a priest's house some ancient records which referred to marriages and deaths in the village of Tayopa.

But other people were now seriously hunting for the Tayopa. John Franklin Lewis, a Mormon who mined in Mexico before the Revolution, spent fifteen years and 80 000 dollars searching for the lost mine. He was unsuccessful, but by way of compensation he discovered in the process a rich gold mine near Bacerac, in Sonora.

In May 1911 Flipper went to Spain to consult the Archivos General de Indias, in the hope of gleaning further information about Tayopa. He discovered several documents, including the inventory mentioned earlier. One record disclosed that the location of the tunnel or vault where the treasure was stored was '2281 *varas* [about 2024 yards] east of the church door, and 63 *varas* [about 57 yards] to the south. The tunnel has a metal door and lock. . . .' Flipper estimated that, at the time when the settlement was abandoned, the stored bullion was worth about £10 million.

Another document that he brought to light gave some directions for placing the mine: 'When standing on the summit of the Cerro de la Campana near the villa de la Conception, look west as the sun sets on the seventh day of March. You will be looking straight towards Tayopa, eight days' journey away.'

Flipper was never able to make use of all the information he uncovered. The Revolution put an end to his work there and he was sent on to Venezuela, never returning to Mexico. So far, the lost Tayopa mine has not been rediscovered and few Americans venture into the harsh, rugged region where it is supposed to be. And, certainly three hundred years' unchecked growth of vegetation will have effectively concealed both the mine and the mission from all but the most careful – and lucky – searcher.

By using the known information, however, it is certainly possible to narrow down the area of search. Subsequent rediscovery of Guaynopa was a piece of good fortune, for it is now sure that Guaynopita lies to the south-east of Guaynopa, up the Rio Chico, and this in turn is of considerable help in enabling us to place the Tayopa.

In 1927 another small clue was found by Carl Sauer of the University of California. While he was immersed in research in the small town of Arizpe, Sonora, he was allowed to see some ancient documents, among which were some marriage banns that had been drawn up by the *cura* or priest of Tayopa.

It was Carl's opinion that Tayopa lay somewhere between Guaynopa and Nacori, an early Spanish settlement and mine founded in far eastern Sonora in 1645.

Another clue was provided in Lieutenant Britton Davis's biography, *The Truth about Geronimo*. In 1885 he led troops into the Sierra Madre on the heels of the wily Apache and finally arrived at the little village of Nacori. There Davis first heard about Tayopa.

'My informant, the white-haired *presidente*, a man of over eighty years of age, told me that his grandfather, who had also lived to be a very old man, had worked the mine as a boy, and that it was in a mountain range to the east of Nacori.' Later, the *presidente* told Davis that 'Here, in Nacori, where we stand, on a still night one could hears the dogs bark and the church bells ring in Tayopa.'

Flipper's document relating to the Cerro de la Campana is yet another pointer to the mine's location. He consulted old mining records to find that the villa de la Conception (mentioned in connection with the hill) was now called Guerrero – today a town of reasonable size, in the State of Chihuahua and some way west of Chihuahua City.

'North-west of it,' states Flipper, 'is a bell-shaped hill and it was at that time called the Cerro de la Campana. Looking towards the sunset in March, Tayopa would lie east of Guasavas and Granados, one of the towns where I saw the Tayopa records. In my opinion, Tayopa lies within the triangle of Guaynopa, Satachi and Guadalupe.' He went on to point out that this relates to one of only two trails which crossed the Sierra Madre in early times, passing Guaynopa and up the Rio Satachi to Guasavas and Granados, and then continuing to Hermosillo. Evidence found by the Mormon, Lewis, suggests that the Tayopa, Guaynopa and Guaynopita formed an elongated triangle.

When Flipper found and examined the documents in the towns of Guasavas and Granados he formed the opinion that 'these records were not brought from a great distance by people who were fleeing for their lives, and they preclude all idea of the Tayopa being south of the Yaqui River, or even south of these two towns'. The fleeing priests, in his opinion, would not have gone north into country where the Indians had risen in rebellion, but would have gone to settlements with sufficient troops or population to defend them.

In 1971 a writer who set out to look for the lost mine described the route he took. His account gives a good idea of the ruggedness of the country, as well as providing one route to the Guaynopa mine. From El Paso in Texas he journeyed by truck to the south-west for some 290 miles, crossing the desert in Chihuahua on a paved road that took him to the old Mormon settlement of Colonia Juarez. Continuing in a south-westerly direction, but on a much rougher road, he drove another eighty miles to the village of Chuhuichupa, a small *pueblo* of about a hundred families. There he hired a guide to take him on the four-day trek into the Guaynopa area.

Heading south-west on the first day, they drove over an old logging trail which ran above the canyon-scarred Rio Bonito, and then descended some 2500 feet into the Rio Guaynopa, where the trail became extremely difficult, sometimes running through the bed of the stream. In the afternoon they could take the truck no further and so changed to horses, making their way downstream to a place called Las Cuadras (twin caves). Here, in the caves, they made camp for the night. The next morning, despite a cold rain which gradually turned to icy sleet, they continued down the canyon until they found a rock ledge by which they crossed to the opposite wall. They climbed the canyon, still moving downstream, and saw the ruins of an Indian *pueblo* which covered several acres.

On the third morning, they persevered in a south-westerly direction, until their journey was halted by the discovery of an ancient Spanish fortress on top of a hill. Here it became apparent why the Tayopa has managed to elude searchers for so long. The guide told them that though he had passed this spot on eight occasions in previous years he had never before observed the fortress. For the rest of the day they continued to follow the river southward.

By the fourth day, they found that the country was getting much rougher. Still riding south, they traversed narrow trails atop almost sheer drops, repeatedly ducking to avoid overhanging cacti, 'whose sword-like thorns would rip your flesh open at the slightest touch'.

At times, there seemed to be no trail to follow and even the horses found it tough going but eventually it led downwards until the canyon cut into the Rio Chico, and below was the Rio Aros, forming the headwaters of the Rio Yaqui. Here, where the Guaynopa stream joined the Rio Chico, they found the old Guaynopa mine tunnelled into the hillside at the bottom of the gorge. On a small flat area cut into the side of the opposite canyon, almost hidden from view, was the old mission. The writer had been within earshot of the lost Tayopa.

The mine was lost and at first unsought for fear of the Apache, but that menace has now long been removed. The last Apache was killed in the Sierra Madres in 1933. Thus, the way is open for anyone who has the time and energy to cross the inhospitable terrain. With three hundred years of dereliction behind it, the church may now be difficult to find, but the amount of treasure that is said to be concealed underneath would certainly make it worth the try.

Here is a copy of the Spanish record which lists the cache. Dated 17 February 1646 it details seventeen mines in the Tayopa area.

A true and positive description of the mining camp Real of Our Lady of Guadalupe of Tayopa, made in January 1646, by the Right Reverend Father Guardian Fray, Francisco Villegas Garsina y Orosco, Royal Vicar-General of the Royal and Distinguished Jesuit Order of Saint Ignacio of Tayopa, and Jesuit of the Great Faculty of the Province of Sonora and Biscalla, whom may God keep long years.

[Here the document indicated the treasure hidden in the church basement vault.]

Four bells, the largest weighing 28 arrobas and 17 pounds [a total of 727 pounds] on which were inscribed TAYOPA. One bell inscribed REMEDIOS. Weight 11 arrobas and 10 pounds. One small bell inscribed PIEDAD. Weight 5 arrobas. These bells were cast in 1603 by the Right Reverend Father Ignacio Maria de Retana.

One high cross of carved silver from the Tayopa mine, weight 1 arroba, 15 pounds, with an attached crucifix of hammered gold from the Paramo placer.

A pair of processional candle holders and six bars of hammered

96

Right : The Great Hall of Tayos is one enormous chamber in the vast complex that runs through the limestone of the Andes. The geometric forms with their exact right angles suggest that if not entirely man-made they have at least been extensively worked. (*Camera Press*)

Below : The beach at Bel Ombre on Mahé Island in the Seychelles. It was here that many pirates fled after the great exodus from Tortuga. The workings, clearly visible in the picture are those of Cruise-Wilkins. (*David Forman*)

Top left: Indians beside the Little Big Horn River. It was near this point that Marsh, Thompson and Foulk buried the shipment of gold. (*Denver Public Library*)

Top right: General Custer in 1865. It seems that in the national outcry that followed the massacre at the battle of the Little Big Horn the valuable shipment of gold that was being guarded was overlooked. (*Mansell Collection*)

Above: Fort Huachuca. While stationed here in 1941 Private Robert Jones stumbled across a fortune in gold and silver ingots. He authenticated the find by selling some gold but was never able to locate the treasure again. (*Denver Public Library*)

Above : Tombstone, Arizona
in 1880 looking much as it
must have done when Red
Curley, Zwing Hunt, Jim
Hughes and John 'Doc' Neal
hid the profits from their
many raids that were not to
be re-discovered until 1941,
only to be lost again.
(*Western Americana Picture
Library*)

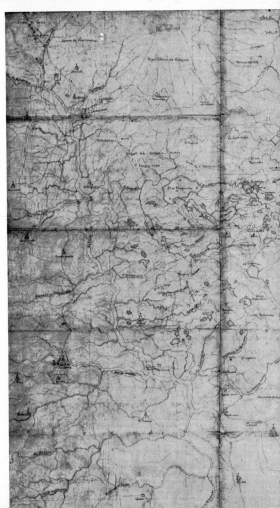

Right : This map of the
Llanganati area dates back
to the early 1800s. Richard
Spruce, a British botanist,
took it from Don Atanasio
Guzman who had died in
1808 having unsuccessfully
hunted for the treasure over
many years. Spruce had
discovered the map while
hunting for the original of
the *Derrotero*. (*Royal
Geographical Society*)

Top left : Percy Harrison Fawcett had this last picture taken in 1911 at Pelechuco before he disappeared in his hunt for the Lost Mines of Muribeca. (*Brian Fawcett*)

Top right : The Apache chief Geronimo. It was the final expulsion of this famous Indian leader that made the re-opening of many of the lost Jesuit mines possible, but the most valuable of them all, the Tayopa mine, still remains shrouded in mystery. (*Western Americana Picture Library*)

Left : This prospector is typical of those to be found throughout Superstition Mountains in the later part of the nineteenth century. Having arrived in town in this state, it was important to hide your cache, taking a little with you so that you could return prosperous to unearth the rest and thus avoid suspicion. Many hid their caches but never returned. (*Arizona Photographic Associates Inc*)

Above : An aerial view of Oak Island. In the gap between the two woods in the foreground can be seen the destruction caused by a succession of attempts to try to recover Captain Kidd's hidden hoard. The use of heavy equipment has removed traces of many of the well documented clues. (*Nova Scotia Communication & Information Centre*)

Right : One of the platforms in the ingenious construction of the pit. (*Nova Scotia Communication & Information Centre*)

Above : The Shepherds of Arcadia, a copy of which was in the possession of Beranger Saunière, proved to be crucial in deciphering part of the abbé's elaborate clues. Is it possible that Poussin who painted the picture with its strange message and uncanny resemblance to Rennes le Château was providing a vital clue to the treasure of the Temple from Jerusalem? (*Lauros-Giraudon*)

Right : This monument in the grounds of Shugborough Hall may provide a further clue to the mystery treasure of Rennes le Château. Poussin's painting has been reversed in the sculpture plaque and the letters OUOSVAVV are clearly visible. Neither the reason for the monument nor the cipher on it have ever been satisfactorily explained. (*National Trust*)

Left : One of the
architectural follies of the
Abbé Saunière built it is
assumed with the fortune
found at Rennes le
Château. (*Art et photo,
Carcassonne*)

Below : The Château des
d'Hautpoul of Rennes
was the home of Marie
de Nègre whose headstone
provided Saunière with a
vital clue to the treasure's
whereabouts. (*Art et
photo, Carcassonne*)

Top : Weaver's Needle is the
strongest clue to locating the Lost
Dutchman mine. Many have died
in the search for a lucrative hoard.
Somewhere perhaps even in this
picture, is the entrance to the mine
with its priceless cache. (*Arizona
Photographic Associates Inc*)

Above : Superstition Mountains are
riddled with old mines one of the
most famous of which is the Lost
Dutchman. Attempts to locate
it have been partially successful but
this picture gives some idea of the
difficult and desolate terrain.
(*Arizona Photographic Associates Inc*)

silver, weighing 4 arrobas, 13 pounds from Santo Niño Mine.

Four incensories of silver and gold plated, weighing 1 arroba, 3 pounds from the Cristo Mine.

In a cut-stone box are stored jewellery. Box is buried in basement under room built of stone and mud, between the church and side of convent and fruit garden.

One large custody with silver bracket, weighing 1 arroba from Santo Niño Mine, with gold glimmer from placer El Paramo and four fine mounted stones from Remedios Mine.

Two silver chalices from the Jesus Maria y Jose Mine, and twelve solid gold cups.

Six gold plates made from Cristo Mine and Purisima Mine, and two large communion plates of gold made from placer El Paramo.

One shrine with four hammered silver columns weighing 4 arrobas from Señor de la Buena Muerto Mine.

Sixty-five cargas [packloads] of silver packed in cow-hide bags, each containing 8 arrobas, 12 pounds.

Eleven cargas of gold from four mines and placer El Paramo, each wrapped in cloth and cow-hide, with a total weight of 99 arrobas [2512 pounds].

Also 183 arrobas of Castilla ore, and 65 arrobas first-class Castilla ore from El Paramo, with a known assay of 22 carats, clean and without mercury.

For the knowledge of our Vicar General, I have written this to inform our Superior.

Left : This sinister ruin is the entrance to Ta Som Temple, Bayon at Angkor. The treasure of Jayavarman was never found when the Siamese sacked the city in 1431. Rumours of a hidden cache have always persisted and the probability is that amongst these awe-inspiring ruins lies a treasure of fabulous richness. (*Douglas Dickins*)

D

The Beale Codes

Codes and ciphers have frequently been used when treasure has been hidden. Secret writing, indeed, is as old as literacy itself: examples of codes or ciphers occur in the Bible, the most widely known being Jeremiah 51 : 41 (A.V.), 'How is Sheshach taken! and how is the praise of the whole earth surprised! how is Babylon become an astonishment among the nations!' Here, the word 'Sheshach' really means 'Babylon'. The The word 'Babel' (i.e. Babylon) has been enciphered by a simple substitution cipher, which the Jews call *Athbash*, and which is explained in detail in the Jewish Cabala.

These simple forms of secret ciphers occur throughout Jewish religious writings, and the idea was later borrowed and enthusiastically employed by the monks of the Middle Ages. Secret writing flourished in Roman times, too, and eventually led to the development of shorthand, though a form of shorthand may have been in use among the Greeks as early as the fourth century B C.

The mysterious Roger Bacon employed ciphers in the thirteenth century, and Geoffrey Chaucer in the fourteenth. In the sixteenth century codes began to make their appearance.

The difference between a code and a cipher is that whereas a cipher is a simple substitution of another letter or symbol for any letter of the alphabet (for example, A = Ø; B = Q; C = 4) a code is formed by employing groups of figures or numbers to represent a word or phrase (gun battery = KQKQKQ; infantry = 669969, and so on).

The art of cryptology has gradually developed and become extremely sophisticated, partly because of its increased use in commerce, but more through its use in military intelligence services. Skill in the art of enciphering, however, has usually been matched by skill in decoding. Sometimes, though, an unbreakable code or cipher has been devised, one which successfully defies the efforts of the most skilful of crypt-analytic experts. One such is contained in an anonymous, untitled volume known as the 'Voyniche Manuscript', which now reposes in the vaults of the Beinecke Rare Book Library at Yale University. Thought to have been written some time in the thirteenth century, this mysterious book has tantalized the world's leading cryptologists since the mid-1600s, and its cipher remains unsolved to this day.

A similar, though less well-known instance, was an unbreak-able code that originated in America in the early nineteenth century. It was devised to pinpoint a large cache of buried treasure and, although the key was lost, the code describing the location of the cache has survived to baffle treasure hunters ever since.

The story began in Virginia in 1817, when thirty men decided to make an exploratory trip into the West. They left Virginia in April and made their way to St Louis, Missouri, the town which was to be their jumping-off point. Their leader was a man named Thomas Jefferson Beale, of unknown age but thought to be about thirty. Beale was over six feet tall with jet black eyes and hair, a dark, swarthy complexion being his most distinguishing feature. He appeared to be unusually strong.

On 19 May the party left St Louis and headed westward, arriving at Santa Fe, New Mexico, on 1 December. Beale and his companions decided to stay in the town until the winter was over.

'Nothing of interest,' wrote Beale later, 'occurred during the winter, and of this little town we soon became heartily tired. We longed for the advent of weather which would enable us to resume our wanderings and our exhilarating pursuits.'

Early in March 1818 a few of the men decided to scout the surrounding countryside. Leaving Santa Fe, they rode north-wards where they found abundant game to hunt. The few days that they had meant to be away stretched into weeks and they were just about to return when they chanced upon an immense herd of buffalo. They quickly made camp in a nearby ravine and began to hunt the animals.

One evening, while they were preparing a meal, a member of the party discovered gold ore in a cleft in the rock quite close to the campsite, which they estimated was 250 miles north of Santa Fe – today in the State of Colorado. Excited by their find, two of the men returned to bring the news to Beale and the others.

'Upon reaching the locality,' wrote Beale, 'I found all as it had been reported and the excitement intense. Everyone was diligently at work with such tools and appliances as they had improvised, and quite a little pile had already accumulated.'

To keep the gold in such wild open country was inviting disaster, and the men therefore decided to have it shipped back to Virginia. A cave near Buford's tavern, in Bedford County, was chosen, as everybody knew it, and in the summer of 1819 Beale and some of the men set out with the precious cargo. When they arrived, in November, they found that local farmers were using the cave to store sweet potatoes and so they were obliged to select an alternative hiding place. Somewhere in the Blue Ridge Mountains they constructed an underground vault in which they cached the gold.

In January 1820 Beale rode into nearby Lynchburg and booked a room at the Washington Hotel, where he soon made the acquaintance of the manager, forty-two-year-old Robert Morriss. Beale stayed until 28 February and then returned to the site of the mine. By now the men had also discovered silver.

In December 1821 Beale made a second deposit at the vault and then wrote down the location of the cache, the amount of treasure in it, and the names of the other twenty-nine men. He devised an unbreakable code with which to encipher the information, using three separate methods. These were written onto sheets labelled '1', '2', and '3' and put into a small but stout iron box.

Beale returned once more in January 1822 to the Washington Hotel and stayed there until April. Before he left he entrusted the box to Morriss, telling the manager that it contained important papers and asking him to care for them until they were called for.

In early May of the same year Beale arrived in St Louis and deposited a letter with a friend. It has never been possible to trace this man but the letter was addressed to Robert Morriss of Lynchburg and marked 'Not to be delivered until June 1832'. It contained the key to Beale's codes.

On 16 May Morriss received a letter from Beale which had been written in St Louis on 9 May. In it Beale said that he would shortly leave St Louis for the western plains to hunt buffalo. He repeated his request that Morriss should take great care of the box, and further instructed that if, after ten years, he or his authorized agent had not retrieved it, then Morriss was to open it. Inside he would find papers that meant nothing without the key to solve them – and this, he explained, was in the hands of a friend who would deliver it in June 1832. With the key Morris would be able to decipher the instructions within the box.

Morriss never heard from Beale again. He had put the box away in his safe and more or less forgotten about it. The year of 1832 came and went. The box was not collected nor was the letter from St Louis received. Not until 1845 did the hotel manager decide to do something about his trust. He had the lock broken open and found inside two letters addressed to himself and several sheets of paper covered with numbers. One of the letters described the finding of the gold, and the subsequent construction of the vault. Dated 4 January 1822, Lynchburg, Va., the letter ended: 'As ten years must elapse before you see this letter, you can conclude, by that time that none of us will be alive. You will then go to the depository and divide its contents into thirty-one equal parts. One of these parts you will keep for your services. The other shares are to be distributed to the parties named in No. 3.'

But without the key Morriss could do nothing and there was no clue to the identity of the mysterious 'friend' in St Louis. Hoping that someone would eventually come forward to claim the box, Morriss returned it to his safe, where it remained untouched for the next seventeen years. The Civil War came, with its three years of bloody upheaval, and this prompted Morriss to make a decision about the strange collection of papers. In 1862, the second year of the war, Morriss, who was now eighty-four, revealed the secret of the iron box to his close friend, James B. Ward. They agreed that, should Ward solve the puzzle and find the treasure, he was to receive half Morriss's share, with the other half being bequeathed to Morriss's surviving relatives. The rest of the treasure was to be held in trust for any claimants that might appear. If the amount was still unclaimed after twenty years, it would then revert wholly to Ward.

Ward, still a young man and encouraged at the prospects, eagerly accepted the coded sheets. He well knew that the chances of the treasure being claimed after a lapse of forty years were hearteningly slight. He began to work on the codes with a zeal that soon developed into an obsession. He ignored the pleas of his wife and the advice of friends, relentlessly continuing with his investigation until his family life suffered and his income dwindled. Finally, after twenty years, almost poverty stricken, he gave up.

In 1885 he collected together all the knowledge of the codes, along with the small success he had enjoyed, and wrote them into a pamphlet which he entitled *The Beale Papers*. It was priced to sell at 50 cents and printed by the Virginian Job Print of Lynchburg. But he was denied even the fruits of this labour for, before it could be distributed for sale, a fire in the printing shop destroyed all but a few copies.

Ward detailed the systems that he employed in trying to crack the codes. He did manage to decipher Code 2, as the pamphlet explains:

My impression was that each number represented a letter. But the different numbers used exceeded the letters of the alphabet. I wondered then, if some document had been used, with each word assigned a different number. With this idea in mind, a test was made, using every book I could produce. By numbering the letters and comparing their numbers with those of the manuscript, I hoped to find the answer. It wasn't until I used the Declaration of Independence that the code began to crack.

Ward explained how he numbered each word of the Declaration from 1 to 1322. When he compared the resulting breakdown with the numbers on Code 2, he realized that he had the right key. He saw the first letter of each word was used to make up the coded context, and he soon had the decoded message in front of him. It read:

I have deposited in the County of Bedford about four miles from Bufords in an excavation or vault six feet below the surface of the ground the following articles belonging jointly to the parties whose names are given in number three herewith. The first deposit consisted of ten hundred and fourteen pounds of gold and thirty-eight hundred and twelve pounds of silver deposited November 1819. The second was made December 1821 and consisted of nineteen hundred and seven pounds of gold and twelve hundred and eighty-eight of silver also jewels obtained in St Louis in exchange to save transportation and valued at thirteen thousand dollars. The above is securely packed in iron pots with iron covers. The vault is roughly lined with stones and the vessels rest on solid stone and are covered with others. Paper number one describes the exact locality of the vault so that no difficulty will be had in finding it.

Now Ward knew exactly what the treasure was and, having made this discovery, thought he had the key to the rest of the papers. But when he applied the method to Codes 1 and 3, he found that the key did not work. In the pamphlet he wrote that he had lost all hope of benefit for himself, but hoped that someone else would try.

Someone else did. His name was Clayton Hart and he was a stenographer who had obtained one of the surviving copies of Ward's pamphlet in 1897. He and his brother George visited James Ward and confirmed with him the story of the treasure. Together they tried for ten years to solve the code, but without success. Finally losing heart they took to working on it only in their spare time.

In December 1924 George happened to read an article about a Colonel George Fabyan, who was an expert at breaking codes. Full of renewed hope, they sent him the papers and asked him if he could crack the codes. On 3 February 1925 Colonel Fabyan replied: 'A code of this character could not be deciphered without the key, regardless of whether one put twenty or forty years on it.' George Hart gave up, but Clayton worked on until his death in 1949.

To date, apart from the one stroke of good fortune enjoyed

by Ward when he stumbled on the key to Code 2, work has been fruitless.

According to the facts of the story, there were thirty men involved, all of whom presumably knew the location of the treasure vault. The code was only used as an assurance that the proceeds would go to dependants, via Morriss, should every single one of the party be killed. You can judge for yourself how improbable it would be that all the men failed to return. And Beale himself could have returned to recover the treasure without telling Morriss about it – although the story depicts Beale as being a man of intelligence and character, hardly likely to be so remiss.

Also, had any of the men survived and yet not known the exact location of the cache, it seems safe to assume that they would have known of the iron box in Morriss's possession and what it contained.

If the treasure still lies in the vault, the modern treasure hunter has a far better chance of finding it by the use of an up-to-date detector. It is only a matter of pinpointing the site of the vault, although it must be admitted that this would be a painstaking process. All available information indicates that it is buried somewhere near the Peaks of Otter, in the Blue Ridge Mountains of Bedford County, Virginia, USA. If you consult the deciphered Code 2, you will see that the site of the vault is said to be four miles from Buford's tavern. Of course, the tavern is no longer there, but at the site of this landmark there now stands the small village of Montvale, which is today located off Highway 460. Once in the area, a local survey map will indicate the arc of search four miles from Montvale.

The only other way of unearthing the cache is to crack that remaining code. In case you would like to try, here is a copy of Code 1.

71 – 194 – 38 – 1701 – 89 – 76 – 11 – 83 – 1629 – 48 – 94 –
63 – 132 – 16 – 111 – 95 – 84 – 341 – 975 – 14 – 40 – 64 –
27 – 81 – 139 – 213 – 63 – 90 – 1120 – 8 – 15 – 3 – 126 –
2018 – 40 – 74 – 758 – 485 – 604 – 230 – 436 – 664 – 582 –
150 – 251 – 284 – 308 – 231 – 124 – 211 – 486 – 225 – 401 –
370 – 11 – 101 – 305 – 139 – 189 – 17 – 33 – 88 – 208 – 193 –
145 – 1 – 97 – 73 – 416 – 918 – 263 – 28 – 500 – 538 – 356 –

117 – 136 – 219 – 27 – 176 – 130 – 10 – 460 – 25 – 485 – 18 –
436 – 65 – 84 – 200 – 283 – 118 – 320 – 138 – 36 – 416 – 280 –
15 – 71 – 224 – 961 – 44 – 16 – 401 – 39 – 88 – 61 – 304 –
12 – 21 – 24 – 283 – 134 – 92 – 63 – 246 – 486 – 682 – 7 –
219 – 184 – 360 – 780 – 18 – 64 – 463 – 474 – 131 – 160 –
79 – 73 – 440 – 95 – 18 – 64 – 581 – 34 – 69 – 128 – 367 –
460 – 17 – 81 – 12 – 103 – 820 – 62 – 116 – 97 – 103 – 862 –
70 – 60 – 1317 – 471 – 540 – 208 – 121 – 890 – 346 – 36 –
150 – 59 – 568 – 614 – 13 – 120 – 63 – 219 – 812 – 2160 –
1780 – 99 – 35 – 18 – 21 – 136 – 872 – 15 – 28 – 170 – 88 –
4 – 30 – 44 – 112 – 18 – 147 – 436 – 195 – 320 – 37 – 122 –
113 – 6 – 140 – 8 – 120 – 305 – 42 – 58 – 461 – 44 – 106 –
301 – 13 – 408 – 680 – 93 – 86 – 116 – 530 – 82 – 568 – 9 –
102 – 38 – 416 – 89 – 71 – 216 – 728 – 965 – 818 – 2 – 38 –
121 – 195 – 14 – 326 – 148 – 234 – 18 – 55 – 131 – 234 – 361 –
824 – 5 – 81 – 623 – 48 – 961 – 19 – 26 – 33 – 10 – 1101 –
365 – 92 – 88 – 181 – 275 – 346 – 201 – 206 – 86 – 36 – 219 –
320 – 829 – 840 – 68 – 326 – 19 – 48 – 122 – 85 – 216 – 284 –
919 – 861 – 326 – 985 – 233 – 64 – 68 – 232 – 431 – 960 –
50 – 29 – 81 – 216 – 321 – 603 – 14 – 612 – 81 – 360 – 36 –
51 – 62 – 194 – 78 – 60 – 200 – 314 – 676 – 112 – 4 – 28 –
18 – 61 – 136 – 247 – 819 – 921 – 1060 – 464 – 895 – 10 –
6 – 66 – 119 – 38 – 41 – 49 – 602 – 423 – 962 – 302 – 294 –
875 – 78 – 14 – 23 – 111 – 109 – 62 – 31 – 501 – 823 – 216 –
280 – 34 – 24 – 150 – 1000 – 162 – 286 – 19 – 21 – 17 – 340 –
19 – 242 – 31 – 86 – 234 – 140 – 607 – 115 – 33 – 191 – 67 –
104 – 86 – 52 – 88 – 16 – 80 – 121 – 67 – 95 – 122 – 216 –
548 – 96 – 11 – 201 – 77 – 364 – 218 – 65 – 667 – 890 – 236 –
154 – 211 – 10 – 98 – 34 – 119 – 56 – 216 – 119 – 71 – 218 –
1164 – 1496 – 1817 – 51 – 39 – 210 – 36 – 3 – 19 – 540 – 232 –
22 – 141 – 617 – 84 – 290 – 80 – 46 – 207 – 411 – 150 – 29 –
38 – 46 – 172 – 85 – 194 – 36 – 261 – 543 – 897 – 624 – 18 –
212 – 416 – 127 – 931 – 19 – 4 – 63 – 96 – 12 – 101 – 418 –
16 – 140 – 230 – 460 – 538 – 19 – 27 – 88 – 612 – 1431 – 90 –
716 – 275 – 74 – 83 – 11 – 426 – 89 – 72 – 84 – 1300 – 1706 –
814 – 221 – 132 – 40 – 102 – 34 – 858 – 975 – 1101 – 84 –
16 – 79 – 23 – 16 – 81 – 122 – 324 – 403 – 912 – 227 – 936 –
447 – 55 – 86 – 34 – 43 – 212 – 107 – 96 – 314 – 264 – 1065 –
323 – 428 – 601 – 203 – 124 – 95 – 216 – 814 – 2906 – 654 –
820 – 2 – 301 – 112 – 176 – 213 – 71 – 87 – 96 – 202 – 35 –
10 – 2 – 41 – 17 – 84 – 221 – 736 – 820 – 214 – 11 – 60 –
760 –.

The New Mexico Cache

Somewhere in the remote high plateau of the north-west corner of New Mexico, USA, lie buried seventeen tons of gold ingots, a treasure that is worth – by today's prices – well over twenty million dollars. This unique cache does not constitute the stolen loot of either pirates or bandits and is only illegal because its owners have contravened the American Gold Reserve Act of 1934.

The story begins in the spring of 1933, when a rich Mexican mine owner, Leon Trabuco, called a meeting of four business acquaintances: a financier, Rafael Borrega, two cattlemen named Don Carlos Sepulvedo and Ricardo Arteaga from Torreon, and Professor Guzman Hilario y Morada, a noted Mexican economist.

Trabuco explained that they were assembled to discuss a rather bold financial opportunity that had been envisaged by Morada. The price of gold in the United States was then 20·66 dollars an ounce and the recent stock market crash and the subsequent depression made it inevitable that the dollar would be devalued. In view of the uncertain conditions then prevailing in Mexico, Morada's plan was to form a syndicate, pool their financial resources and buy as much gold as they could possibly afford. They would then ship it secretly across the border and wait for devaluation. The dollar price of gold would rise and they would be able to sell at a handsome profit.

They soon reached an agreement, for there was no shortage of cash. Borrega was a private banker who dealt in investments and boasted clients who entrusted him with large sums of

106

money. Sepulvedo and Arteaga were both millionaire cattlemen, and Trabuco himself owned a veritable empire of mines in the Sierra Madres. Morada was the only one not to participate financially. He was there purely as an adviser.

Each man pledged himself to buy a certain amount of gold. Together they acquired an old *hacienda* just outside Mexico City to use as a storehouse or stockpile. Trabuco, meanwhile, went to the United States to select a safe depository for the gold, but this proved to be more difficult than he anticipated. He inspected bank vault facilities in several major cities – Los Angeles, San Antonio, Phoenix – but eventually decided against them on the grounds that it would be impossible to move such a large amount of the metal into a bank without arousing curiosity in the minds of the employees. Trabuco had good reason to be cautious, for the syndicate's secret hoard had now reached the staggering total of seventeen tons.

Storage buildings, furniture warehouses and similar premises were carefully considered, and all ultimately rejected. Finally, Trabuco made up his mind to bury the gold in one of the remote areas in the US where it could be safely hidden. He chartered a private plane, a Cessna owned by ex-stunt flyer William Elliot, and carried out a series of aerial surveys until he located a suitable spot to cache the gold. Having assessed that Elliot was an adventurous character and willing to take a risk, Trabuco divulged the true intention of the flights. Elliot agreed to smuggle the gold bars by air – for a price. The location of the cache was decided and Elliot flew Trabuco back to Mexico City.

An immediate meeting of the syndicate was called and it was agreed that Elliot was necessary for the success of the plan. He was to be paid for each delivery of ingots to the site of the cache, but he was not to know the exact location of the hole in which the gold was buried.

Trabuco returned to the States and purchased a one-ton pick-up truck, which he drove to the landing site, a flat *mesa* high up in the desolate country of San Juan County, New Mexico, where he set up camp. He then wired Elliot with orders to begin ferrying the gold. To shift such a quantity of gold must have taken a number of flights, probably made at night and using a variety of routes, but there is no record of Elliot's plane being detected by either the US or the Mexican authorities. When the last shipment was made and the Cessna had took off again, Trabuco and two helpers loaded the gold into the pick-up and ferried it in several journeys to the hole in which it was to be buried. Only these three people knew the secret location of the hoard.

Trabuco and his two employees returned to Mexico. Now all they had to do was sit back and wait for devaluation.

The first snag arose on 31 January 1934, when President Roosevelt established the Gold Reserve Act. Every holder of gold or gold notes was required by law to turn them over to the Treasury in exchange for paper currency. Except for a few minor exemptions, heavy penalties could be incurred by those who failed to comply. There was a period of grace allowed for everyone to make the change. The syndicate held a hurried meeting to discuss this new complication, but decided to sit tight and sell to a private buyer as soon as devaluation took place.

When the Gold Reserve Act came into force, the paper dollar – as Morada had foreseen – was devalued and the price of gold immediately rose to 35 dollars an ounce. The syndicate was jubilant: they had now increased their original investment by eight million dollars!

Borrega, the banker, had been insistent that they sell before the legal period of grace expired, but he was outvoted. On Morada's advice, they waited, since he averred that he foresaw yet another rise in gold prices – and the syndicate would make still more profit.

In 1939 Borrega died suddenly as a result of a heart attack. It was then that the syndicate hit the second snag, for it was discovered that Borrega had been systematically embezzling funds from his rich clients and giving them dividends from their own capital. Investigators were unable to trace several million dollars diverted by Borrega some years ago. The remaining three members of the syndicate realized where Borrega had obtained the funds to purchase his share of the gold, and now saw only too clearly why he had been so anxious to sell. Trabuco and the others saw that it would be most inadvisable to try and dispose of the cache while the Borrega investigation was in progress, so they sat silent and watched the period of grace slip by and expire.

In February 1940 Ricardo Arteaga was killed – gored to death by one of the prize fighting bulls which he bred. Some months later Don Carlos Sepulvedo, together with Mexican film actress Rita Actones, was killed instantly in a head-on collision on the highway between Taxo and Acapulco.

When America entered the Second World War, Elliot joined the Air Force and became a bomber pilot. He was killed in 1944 when his plane was shot down over Germany, having presumably never disclosed any information regarding his part in the hiding of the gold. By now Morada had also died and Trabuco was the sole surviving member of the syndicate; he now began an active effort to sell the hoard. He went to the United States and tried to negotiate with various banks, who refused to have anything to do with such a large amount of illegal gold. Returning to Mexico, he approached a millionaire Swedish industrialist, Axel Wenner-Gren, but was turned down. He then approached a Gestapo chief, Schmitt, who had got out of a beaten Fatherland just in time, it seemed. Schmitt indicated that the German government would be willing to buy, but lost interest as soon as he learned that the gold was still in the United States.

Rumours of the hoard were now spreading, for Trabuco himself was approached by an expatriate Rumanian banker, Ivan Nasicecu, who wanted to buy the gold on behalf of the ex-King of Rumania, Carol II. King Carol was residing in Mexico at that time, eagerly awaiting permission to take up permanent residence in the United States. Though the US government seemed loath to grant the exiled king an entry permit, their hearts might be softened by a bribe of such large amounts of gold. Nasicecu quietly negotiated with Treasury officials in Washington to find out if there was any prospect of an agreement being reached, but he was turned down so definitely that he returned to Mexico with the opinion that it was useless to continue with the project. Furthermore, Nasicecu's approach to the Treasury triggered off a full-scale investigation by secret service agents, which (except for uncovering the details here) led nowhere.

For Trabuco the situation was becoming impossible and he made one more desperate attempt to approach the US government, this time through an intermediary, for he could no longer enter the US without running the risk of being arrested. In the autumn of 1952 a prominent Los Angeles political leader, E. George Luckey, revealed to the US secret service that he had been approached in 1950 by a California public relations man, Bruce Clews, and an attorney, Prentiss Moore, and asked to help arrange the sale of the cache to the United States mint in San Francisco. Clews stated that he had been approached in the matter by Los Angeles businessman Isadore M. Nobel and a mining engineer named Martin Hougen. Hougen, holding power of attorney from the legal owner, sought to sell the gold through an escrow set up with the First National Bank of Ontario in California, where he placed on file an affidavit that he had actually seen the gold. This information was forthcoming as a result of the Federal Grand Jury investigation into the affair in October 1952.

The case had a strange ending, for it was suddenly dropped. None of the transcripts was made available to the public and the whole business was covered in a cloud of bureaucratic secrecy. Today, the whereabouts of Trabuco are unknown. He disposed of his mines in the late 1950s and retired, to spend much of his time abroad. He was last known to have visited Mexico in 1962. Over the intervening years, his two helpers have died, thus leaving him the only one who knows the exact location of the cache. If he is still alive today, Trabuco must be in his eighties.

Nothing stands in the way of anyone who wants to search for this cache, and since the Federal investigation in 1952 many have tried. It is remotely possible that the US secret service has located the gold and secretly disposed of it. Possible but improbable, because so much gold would not go unnoticed if it was brought on to the market. Should the cache be discovered by a lucky treasure hunter, and should he try and dispose of it illegally, he would find it much too hot to handle. All the odds are that the gold is still where Trabuco buried it.

Available information tells that it is in the remote north-west corner of New Mexico, where the boundaries of that state meet those of Arizona, Utah and Colorado. It is high country, about 7000 feet, and it seems likely that the spot that Trabuco picked would be west of the Ute Mountain Indian Reservation, close to Shiprock Peak and Route 504. There is the fact to consider that the one-ton pick-up had to make a number of journeys in order to move seventeen tons of ingots across very rough country, so it could not have been taken far from the actual landing site selected for the Cessna. The evidence is that the ingots were not buried in a cave, but in a hole – and that they were all buried within a day.

The disclosure by Martin Hougen that he actually saw the gold would have to be thoroughly checked by any would-be treasure hunter. Did he see the actual cache? If he did, then the information would almost certainly have been passed on to the secret service. Or did he see only a sample of the gold, and if so, how was it obtained from the cache? There is no doubt in the mind of anyone who has examined the evidence relating to this story that the cache is still where Trabuco buried it.

Captain Kidd, The Oak Island Money Pit and the Jokoate Hoard

Four miles off the shore of Nova Scotia lies a small island which is inextricably linked with the name of Captain William Kidd. Over the last 170 years it has echoed and rung to the sound of treasure hunters' machinery – from the days of the pick and shovel in 1795 to those of the sophisticated drilling machines and underwater TV cameras which are used today. This insignificant blob of land is known as Oak Island, and there is evidence that it was once the stronghold of pirate bands from the Caribbean. For several reasons it was the ideal location for a hideout.

The island lies at a latitude of 44 degrees 31 minutes North and 64 degrees 18 minutes West, at the head of Mahone Bay and close to the mainland, from which it is separated by a narrow channel. The Tancook Islands completely obscure it from the open sea and protect the bay's 240 square miles of water from the storms of the Atlantic. The east end of the island is formed of limestone, gypsum and sandstone, and it seems that there was once a natural sink or blow-hole, which ended in a large natural chamber, some 200 feet below the surface. This sink-hole must have provided a heaven-sent hideyhole for the plunder of early seventeenth-century freebooters, who could rest safe in the knowledge that they were out of the sight of prying eyes aboard passing shipping, while the mainland was not then settled.

It has not been conclusively established that Kidd himself was definitely associated with Oak Island, but clues uncovered in this century strongly support the theory. Kidd was born when the pirate colony on Tortuga was well established, and it is believed that around 1664 he possessed information about the island hideout. He drew a chart of an island which resembled Oak Island in several important details, and then hid the map in a secret compartment of his sea chest in the year 1668. There it remained hidden until 1929. Three other charts of the same island were later found to have been drawn by Kidd, all probably penned in the same period. Naturally, the locations given were not the true ones but all the charts were concealed in the same way.

Not much is known about Kidd's early life and the first documented reference to him is his marriage in 1689, to a wealthy widow in New York. It is known that he commanded a privateer in the West Indies in 1690 and that some of his crew were former pirates but in 1695 he was given a privateering commission to clear the pirates from the Indian Ocean. His ship was the *Adventure Galley*, and it was in the course of this voyage that – technically at least – Kidd turned pirate, for he failed to bring his prizes to port as the law required. Following his arrest in Boston, £14000 worth of loot was unearthed on Gardiners Island, New York. He was sent to England for trial and hanged at Wapping, London, on 23 May 1701.

On the night before his execution, Kidd wrote to the Speaker of the House of Commons the letter which gave birth to the legend of the treasure hoard thereafter connected with his name.

In my proceedings in the Indies, I have lodged goods and treasure to the Value of one hundred thousand pounds, which I desiere the Government may have the benefit of, in order thereto I shall desiere no manner of liberty but to be kept prisoner on board such shipp as may be appointed for that purpose and only give the necessary directions and in case I faile therein I shall desiere no favour but to be forthwith executed according to my sentence.

It is believed that, when his wife was allowed to visit him in prison for the last time, Kidd gave her a piece of paper on which he had written some figures. The paper was seized and examined but nothing could be made of the cryptic numbers.

It was much later realized that the figures corresponded very closely with the nautical bearing of Oak Island.

Careful sifting of evidence and clues, brought to light in later years, seems to indicate that an unknown band of men came to Oak Island in about 1704. Making use of the natural vault at the bottom of the shaft, they cached a sizable treasure, probably the collective proceeds of an era of freebooting which was rapidly coming to an end. The engineering expertise which was applied to concealing the treasure is brilliant. First they dammed back the sea in a nearby cove and then dug a pair of small tunnels downwards at a slight angle, and lined to intersect the main tunnel, one at the 110-foot level, and the other at 150 feet. Then they filled up the main shaft to the 100-foot level, just above the higher of the flood tunnels. Here, they laid a platform on which, it is thought by later experts, they could rest the treasure. The main shaft was then completely filled in, incorporating a series of airtight platforms constructed at almost every ten feet. The final act was to remove the dam from the entrance to the flood tunnels and let the water in. The sea filled the lower levels of the main shaft but, owing to the airtight seal, could rise no further than the 100-foot level, just below the treasure cache. Should anyone attempt to dig down into the shaft without first reconstructing the dam at the entrance of the flood tunnels, the airtight seal would be broken and the sea would rise to find its own level and thus cover up the treasure cache.

Having performed this masterpiece of mining engineering, these unknown adventurers went their way and Oak Island lapsed into obscurity. Nothing more is heard until 1763, when the few families who had settled in the nearby town of Chester, just across the bay, noticed 'strange lights and fires on the island'. No one dared investigate.

In the summer of 1795 a sixteen-year-old boy, Daniel McGinnis, paddled across the channel to the island and set about exploring it. Roaming through the trees on the southeastern end, he found an ancient path which led up a slight slope into a wide clearing, in the centre of which stood a gnarled old oak tree, quite apart from the rest of the woods. The boy happened to notice that a branch, some sixteen feet from the ground, had been lopped off and bore the marks of old rope scores. Looking down, he saw that the branch overhung a circular depression in the ground.

The area's legendary tales of pirates came flooding into his mind and he hurried home to tell his friends the story. The next day he returned with John Smith, aged twenty, and thirteen-year-old Anthony Vaughn, who soon reached the same conclusions as McGinnis. On their next trip they brought the necessary tools and began to excavate the pit. Once the loose earth was cleared, they found themselves in a regular shaft of about thirteen feet wide and, on digging to a depth of twenty feet, they uncovered three platforms, one of flagstones and two of oak logs. At thirty feet, they encountered yet another platform of oak logs, and then realized that the job was too big for them, so they reluctantly shelved the project until they could recruit help.

Nine years later, Smith, Vaughan and McGinnis found the backers they required and formed a syndicate which started work in 1804. They dug right down to the ninety-eight-foot level before the sea water seeped in. Rising to the level of the surrounding ocean, it flooded the shaft to within thirty-three feet of the top. Digging was abandoned.

The pit lay undisturbed for nearly forty years, but the irresistible lure of treasure triumphed and another syndicate was formed, but the outcome was similar. New shafts were sunk alongside the original, only to be flooded in the same way. However, the syndicate kept trying and five years later they were able to uncover the secret of the flood tunnels, but by that time their capital was exhausted and they were forced to cease operating. Throughout the ensuing years, various other companies were formed and work was carried out, all without success.

In 1878 a mysterious Captain Allen appeared in Chester and created an interesting diversion. He hired a boat and searched the nearby waters for two summers, frequently consulting an old map, but without disclosing his objective. Scrupulously following the bearings on his map, he consistently missed Oak Island by a very narrow margin. At the end of his second summer's search he disappeared and was never seen again.

In 1897 a Captain John Welling, scratching about in the undergrowth on the south shore of the island, uncovered a large triangular figure made out of rocks embedded in the earth. It was found that a central arrow across the triangle – like a simulated theodolite – pointed directly at the mouth of the Money Pit, as it had now become known.

Within the year work was again started, and four or five more shafts were bored before the company concerned ran out of funds. In 1909 another attempt was made by one Captain Harry L. Bowdoin of New York, a personal friend of the future President Franklin D. Roosevelt, who paid a visit to the island. Bowdoin's company worked for two years on the project before finally giving up, and Bowdoin himself eventually returned to New York declaring that 'there never was a pirate or any other treasure in the Money Pit on Oak Island'.

The next clue in the search for the treasure came in 1929, when Hubert Palmer, a retired lawyer living in Eastbourne, Sussex, purchased from a London dealer a heavy seventeenth-century oak bureau, which bore a brass plate inscribed 'Captain William Kidd – Adventure Galley – 1669'. Palmer was an avid collector of pirate relics who knew that furniture of this period often contained secret compartments and therefore examined the bureau carefully. He found three hiding places unknown to the previous owner, but all were empty. He searched further and in so doing, broke one of the runners off the lid; inside he found a narrow brass tube around which was wrapped a tightly rolled piece of parchment. It was a chart of an island bearing the words 'China Sea', and the initials 'W.K.' It was dated 1669 but gave no clue to the island's location.

Intrigued, Palmer intensified his search for other Kidd relics, and two years later in 1931, he bought an old sea chest from a very reliable source. Carved upon the lid was the skull and crossbones, and the words 'Captain Kidd, His Chest'. A false bottom in the chest revealed a book dated 1662, underneath which was a faded piece of parchment bearing a map of the same unidentified island. In 1932 Palmer found another similar map, and in 1934 yet another larger drawing of the island, this time more detailed than the previous three. This last map provided a totally different set of directions, and was found inside a chest which bore the words 'William and Sarah Kidd, Their Box'. All were later authenticated and photographed by British Museum experts, and the writing on them was compared to known examples of Kidd's own hand-writing preserved in the Public Records Office in London. They were found to be identical. Hubert Palmer died in 1950. He had been unable to trace the island depicted in the charts: the words 'China Sea' had been enough to throw him off the scent.

In the intervening years various companies bored into the sandy soil around what was now left of the Money Pit. By 1967 the east end of the island had been completely devastated and many valuable clues had disappeared. Even the stone triangle found by Captain Welling was gone. In 1970 the Triton Company was formed, and they brought with them on to the island many highly sophisticated pieces of equipment in an all-out effort to put an end, once and for all, to the legend of the pit. A year later, a large cavity was found at the 212-foot level. An underwater TV camera was carefully lowered to reveal the remains of some old logs lying on the floor of the chamber, more than forty feet deeper than any other treasure hunter had probed before. The *Halifax Herald Chronicle* report on the find states:

A series of pictures show faint outlines of what project manager Da Blakenship says he is certain are three chests, one having a handle on the end and a curved top. Beside another of the chests or boxes, he says, is some sort of tool, not unlike a pick-axe. . . . A more gruesome revelation by the camera probing the same cell was the appearance on the monitor of a human hand, partly clenched, suspended in water. Startled by what he saw, Mr Blakenship said he summoned all his workers, one by one, into the shack housing the television monitor. Each man confirmed that the hand, still covered with flesh, had what looked like a slash mark across the back, while below the mark the mangled flesh suggested that it had been torn or chopped from the wrist.

Experts came to the conclusion that, under certain conditions, it would be possible for human remains to be preserved embedded in the kind of clay to be found at great depths on Oak Island.

One month later, a team of divers were lowered 235 feet into the vast chamber or cavern which extends beneath the Money Pit, but nothing was reported that either confirmed or denied the finding of the three chests. There was one piece of information which further serves to emphasize the lengths to which the unknown constructors of the pit went. During the drilling of a modern shaft to allow the passage of the divers, the engineers bored through yet another flood tunnel at a depth of 212 feet. Rocks from the beach had been used in its construction.

One last small incident occurred in March 1972. A Mr P. J. Mallon from Belfast visited the island and discovered a stone triangle similar to that which had been found by Captain Welling. Mallon's triangle, however, lacks a half circle of stones which is a feature of the other, and is situated 480 feet south-east of the Money Pit. It does not point at the original shaft, but at another tunnel which runs between the main shaft and the shore.

Opinions have always conflicted as to whether Captain Kidd was ever connected with the Money Pit and one fact is quite clear. He had no time to visit Nova Scotia between his return from the Indian Ocean and his transportation to England. If he ever concealed a treasure there, it must have been early in his career. But the Money Pit was thought to have been constructed in 1704, after Kidd was hanged, because in 1965 Robert E. Restall, a fifty-six-year-old former circus and stunt rider who was working at the pit, found a stone inscribed with the date 1704. It seems very flimsy evidence on which to base hypotheses, especially as it is not stated whether the stone was actually found *in* the pit and (even if it was), it could easily have been thrown into the pit at a later date.

Kidd's maps add very little to the solution of the mystery. One of the smaller maps bears the cryptic clues:

515 SE and by 50 N
36 NE 36 NE. Rocks
3 feet by 3 feet by four.

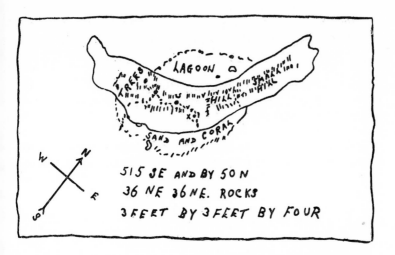

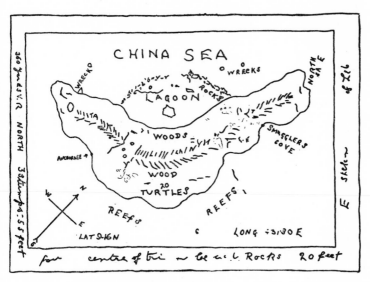

Above: the Kidd–Palmer map found in a sea chest.

Below: This version of the Kidd–Palmer chart was found in the chest marked 'William and Sarah Kidd, Their Box'.

The larger is the more interesting. This is the chart that bears the words 'China Sea'. Around the edges are the following clues which, due to fading are unfortunately incomplete.

> 360 yards V R. North. 3 stumps: 55 feet.
> For . . . centre of tri[angle] . . . Rocks 20 feet.
> E skele[to]n . . . of L(1)6

Below the outline of the island is inscribed this apparently meaningless bearing (the figure 4 is indistinct):

$$\text{Lat 9.16 N . . . Long 4 31.30 E}$$

This chart was probably the last drawn up by Kidd and since it was found in the chest marked 'William and Sarah', it seems logical to assume that he hid it there some time after his marriage in 1689. Perhaps the Money Pit was constructed when those 'lights and fires' were seen in 1763, and certainly no later. But the clues and directions on Kidd's chart refer to a cache hidden well before these dates and one must assume that, when the unknown engineers came to construct the pit, not only could they have altered or erased Kidd's clues, but either moved or relocated that treasure as well.

Does the chart in fact refer to Oak Island at all? Here there are some relevant pieces of evidence. In the bottom centre of the drawing of the island appears the cryptic message '20 turtles', and this I believe is derived from the old nautical term 'to turn turtle', which needs no explanation. If we follow this veiled suggestion and turn the map upside-down, taking the top of the page to indicate north, then we find that the shape and position of the island depicted so closely resemble Oak Island as to be almost unmistakable.

The three wrecks marked are at roughly the correct positions where old Mahone Bay fishermen have located the skeletons of ancient vessels. One difference between it and Oak Island is that the chart depicts a chain of small rocks encircling a lagoon. However, a lagoon did once exist on Oak Island and can still be discerned in some aerial photographs. The anchorage position is identical with Oak Island's best anchorage position, and – it may be sheer coincidence – among the pen marks and scrawls which have been made to represent either trees or hills, appear the letters 'O A K'. Is this accident or design?

There is also flimsy evidence that Kidd may have sailed as far as the China Seas during his period in the Indian Ocean area, and this gives rise to the other tale of this famous captain's treasure. In 1952 some Japanese fishermen were caught in a storm and hurriedly took shelter in a bay on the island of Jokoate, the most northerly island in a group which stretches from the south end of Japan down to Formosa. This chain is called the Luchu Islands (or Ryuku). Jokoate was at that time a desolate, rock-strewn spot, which once had strategic significance during the Second World War when American soldiers used it as a base. The fishermen explored the area and were interested to find carved on a rock face some drawings of a horned animal.

This find was subsequently reported and came to the attention of a Japanese scholar named Masahiro Nagashima, who organized an expedition to the island to examine the carvings for himself. Nagashima had heard that the famous Captain Kidd was reputed to have sometimes used the primitive drawing of a goat (or kid – a pun on his name) as a signature and he assumed that the cache indicated in the 'China Sea' map may well lie on the island.

Nagashima had previously made a study of the old documents and maps relating to the pirate's exploits and there is a strange legend connected with the island on which the vast treasure was found. It was here, the story goes, that three pillars of pure gold had once stood, a kind of prehistoric shrine which had been removed by 'a god from the lap of the sea monster'. Could this have been Kidd, and could there be any connection with the 'three stumps' indicated on Kidd's map?

Nagashima easily found the spot described by the fishermen and made a thorough search. He managed to force an entrance to a cave which was almost entirely concealed by an overgrowth of briar, and there before his eyes lay a heap of old iron boxes. When he opened them he discovered a fortune in gold and silver coin, which was subsequently valued at £30 million. The treasure was transported to Tokyo with the least possible publicity and nothing further was heard of it, but in September 1952 newspapers reported that the Japanese police were looking for Nagashima, who is alleged to have disappeared without a trace, taking the treasure with him.

While Jokoate has given up its treasure the Money Pit has so far yielded nothing – though this will never deter treasure hunters, their syndicates or their investors. The author of a book on the subject, Rupert Furneaux, has called it 'the costliest treasure hunt ever', and he may well be right, especially if Captain Kidd's treasure disappeared with Masahiro Nagashima, which would leave only the 1763 cache.

The Sacambaya Cache

In the Cochabamba Valley of Bolivia, only a hundred miles from La Paz, the site of the old fortress-monastery of Plazuela lies where the River Khato flows into the Sacambaya. Founded by the Jesuits in 1635, it quickly developed into one of their most important strongholds and a central receiving point for the output of the mines in the surrounding hills. These included the famous Tres Tertilias and El Carmen mines, reputedly the richest in South America.

When the order for the Jesuits' expulsion came in 1767, the Fathers refused to believe that it would be implemented. They continued to mine, stockpiling the yield and merely suspending the shipments, confident that the Pope would obtain a reprieve for them. As time passed, however, they realized that Charles III of Spain was determined to see the order carried out, and that only the remoteness of their monastery had saved them so far. Bitter and angry, they held council at which they voted to conceal their accumulated riches. Later, they thought they could return, recover the hidden hoard and use it to further their ambition to found a Jesuit colony in South America.

With virtually unlimited Indian labour at their disposal, they built a great cache near the monastery. Over a period of two years they secreted a vast hoard and then completely erased all traces of the mine workings and the tracks leading to them. When the Spanish soldiers crossed the Andes in 1778 with explicit orders to deport the Jesuits and confiscate their gold, they arrived to find the great monastery deserted and not a trace of the gold. In the hope of extracting information they caught a few Indians and tortured them, but with no success. Eventually the soldiers were compelled to leave empty-handed.

One of the fleeing priests, Father Gregorio San Roman, had a brother who held the post of Prefect in the Peruvian city of Callao and on his way out of the country Gregorio paid him a visit and recounted the whole story. At this meeting a document was drawn up detailing the amount of treasure, how it was concealed and its location. This document, which was kept in trust by the brother after Gregorio's departure, is the vital clue in the story of the Sacambaya cache, and it is therefore set out here in full.

There is a hill on the left bank of the Rio Sacambaya opposite the Monastery of Plazuela. It is steep and covered with dense forest. The top is flat and with long grass growing. In the middle of the long grass there is a large stone shaped like an egg, so big that it took five hundred Indians to place it there. If you dig underneath this stone for five *cordas* [an old Spanish marine measure – one *corda* is thought to be the equivalent of 22 feet 7 inches] you will find the roof of a large cave which it took five hundred Indians two and a half years to hollow out. The roof is twenty-four *cordas* long and there are two compartments and a long narrow passage leading from the room on the east side to the main entrance two hundred *cordas* away. On reaching the door you must exercise great care in opening. The door is a large iron one and inside to the right, near the wall, you will find an image of the Madonna, made of pure gold, three feet high, the eyes of which are two large diamonds; this image was placed there for the good of mankind. If you proceed along the passage you will find in the first room thirty-seven heaps of gold, and many gold and silver ornaments and precious stones. On entering the second room you will find in the right-hand corner a large box clamped with iron bars; inside this box are ninety thousand Duros Reales in silver money and thirty bags of gold. Distributed in the hollows on either side of the tunnel and in the two rooms are, altogether, one hundred and sixty heaps of gold, of which the value has been estimated at sixty million Duros Reales. Great care must be taken on entering these rooms, as enough poison to kill a regiment of the King has been laid about. The walls of the two rooms have been strengthened by large blocks of granite; from the roof downwards the distance is five *cordas* more. The top of the roof is portioned off in three distinct esplanades and the whole has been covered for a depth of five *cordas* with earth and stone.

When you come to a place twenty feet high, with a wall so wide that two men can easily ride abreast, cross the river and you will find the monastery, church and other buildings.

Some idea of the value of the hoard may be gained when it is realized that in 1928 it was estimated to be worth £12 million.

In the years after Simón Bolívar ousted the Spaniards in 1824 a number of efforts were made to unearth the fabulous treasure of Plazuela. The most notable of these was an expedition mounted by the then President of Bolivia, General Mariano Melgarejo. In 1865 he arrived at the site with a large force of soldiers, but though a number of holes were dug the cache was not located. The many other treasure seekers who swarmed to the spot were likewise doomed to failure, for they lacked the information in the San Roman document and the Jesuits had hidden their hoard with great care.

When Gregorio's brother died the treasure document was passed on to his heirs and so by the close of the nineteenth century, it came into the hands of a daughter of the family, Corina San Roman. Having always been rich, the family had made no attempt to recover the hoard, even after it was apparent that the Jesuits would never return to collect it. They were satisfied to keep in touch with the hiding place through an Indian family named Ampuera, who lived in the village of Cuti just a few miles from the monastery; the Ampueras were able to assure the San Romans that, despite the efforts of the many seekers, the treasure still lay undisturbed.

In the early 1900s Corina San Roman decided that the cache should be recovered and to this end she approached Cecil H. Prodgers, a mining engineer well known in Bolivia at the time. Giving him the information in the document and the promise of a share in the treasure, she commissioned him to recover the Jesuit hoard. For three years, during 1905 to 1907, Prodgers spent the whole of the dry seasons at Plazuela, but without success. Finally his health failing, he was forced to abandon the search and returned to England. In his subsequent book, *Adventures in Bolivia*, he described his fruitless hunt. His information he passed to another mining man, Dr Edgar

Sanders, knowing that his own health would never allow him to return to Bolivia, and asked Sanders to fulfil the responsibility to Corina San Roman.

Meanwhile, in the years after Prodgers left the site, hopeful seekers continued to arrive at the monastery. Even the legendary Colonel Fawcett paid a visit during his 1913 trek through Bolivia and in his memoirs recounts how he easily found the old, broken walls of the monastery and, not far away, six or eight open holes. There were also other workings, he reported, that looked as if holes had been dug and filled in again. Fawcett was extremely sceptical of treasure stories but he had been persuaded to visit the site after meeting a Cornishman who had already been excavating for the treasure. This Cornishman told Fawcett that he had knowledge of the hoard through an Englishman with whom he had been a partner and, although Fawcett mentions no names, this may well have been Prodgers. According to the Cornishman's story, they had found definite traces which led them to believe that they were on the right track, but quarrels had broken up the partnership and the Cornishman had been left to work at the site alone. Subsequently, he claimed, he had discovered the entrance to the treasure chamber but then his funds had run out. Asked to supply capital in return for a share, Fawcett declined, for he was more interested in his search for pre-Inca ruins.

In 1925 Dr Edgar Sanders arrived at Plazuela to begin some preliminary investigations. He had with him a copy of the San Roman document, and with it a distinct advantage over previous seekers (except Prodgers) for they had to rely on local tradition which erroneously stated that the treasure was hidden in a hill called Negro Muerto on the right bank of the river – hence Corina San Roman's certainty that the hoard still lay untouched.

Sanders spent two dry seasons at the site and eventually uncovered what he was convinced was the entrance tunnel mentioned in the document. In the season of 1926 he found a silver crucifix in the tunnel and, soon afterwards, came upon a stone wall blocking its entire width. Made of loose, uncemented stones, this wall proved to be no obstacle, but after the first layer had been taken down, Sanders came to a stone receptacle with a rotting wooden interior. The casing crumbled to the touch, revealing a roll of parchment. Sanders slowly translated the Spanish aloud.

You who reach this place, withdraw. This spot is dedicated to God Almighty and the one who dares to enter, a dolorous death awaits him in this world and eternal condemnation in the world he goes to. The riches that belong to God our Master are not for humans. Withdraw and you will live in peace and the blessing of the Master will make your life sweet and you will die rich with the goods of this world. Obey the command of God Almighty our Master in life and in death. In the Name of God, the Father, the Son and the Holy Ghost. Amen.

Although this powerful conjuration affected Sanders not the slightest, the Indian labourers were completely terrified and refused to work in the tunnel any further. Sanders later submitted the parchment to the British Museum who formed the opinion that it was undoubtedly genuine.

It was during this period that Sanders became convinced that the document, while essentially correct, contained some erroneous clues. His impression was that it had been written, not by Gregorio, but by the brother using Gregorio's oral description – and that unintentional misconceptions of the writer made some of the clues misleading. For instance, the document instructs the seeker to dig underneath the egg-shaped stone to find the entrance to the tunnel. Sanders came to the conclusion that the huge stone was placed there merely to mark the hill in which the treasure chamber lay, and that the entrance tunnel really began some 1500 yards away in the direction of the monastery.

Sanders did not preclude the possibility that the document was deliberately incomprehensible, a suspicion which was not allayed by the discovery of an artificial pile of rock which he christened the Square Stone Heap. 618 feet long by 120 feet wide, this man-made structure lay – at a rough measurement – just 200 *cordas* away from the egg-shaped stone. This fact led Sanders to believe that the Square Stone Heap was the roof of the treasure cavern. Convinced that he was near to finding the Jesuit millions, he leased the grounds around the monastery from their owner, Señor Jacinto Aguilar, and secured a contract to excavate until the end of 1928.

Feeling that the £6000 he had spent on this first expedition had not been wasted, Sanders returned to England and published a pamphlet entitled 'The Story of the Jesuit Gold Mines in Bolivia and of the Treasure Hidden by the Sacambaya River'. Using this as a promotional lever, he formed a syndicate to raise enough money for a more ambitiously equipped expedition. His hopes were realized when syndicate members provided £20000 with which the Sacambaya Exploration Company was formed. On 1 March 1928 Sanders and twenty-two others sailed from Liverpool. With them went forty-five tons of equipment, including four pneumatic drill compressors, two electric generators, six cranes, a hydraulic pump, a circular saw with engine, two winches, two Morris six-wheel tractors and 1000 gallons of petrol.

The conditions of the journey from La Paz to the Sacambaya were appalling. In the last thirty-two miles they were obliged to ford the River Khato no less than forty-two times, man-handling the heavy equipment with block and tackle. Once at the site, they set to work, one party on the tunnel and another, larger party on the Square Stone Heap.

The first disappointment came when, after ten days' work, the tunnel suddenly came to a blank end, Sanders concluded that it had been a blind lead set to waste the time of treasure seekers. Meanwhile the work on the Square Stone Heap dragged on with no sign of success. In September yet another tunnel into the Heap was started, but by October the rains had come and the pit was being flooded constantly. By November they were forced to give up. On their return to England the Sacambaya Exploration Company went into voluntary liquidation. During the eight months that the expedition had worked at the site, they had blasted and cleared over fifty thousand tons of earth and rock without so much as a sign of the treasure.

Sanders had learned a great deal of the history of Prodgers and a supposed partner of Prodgers – a man named Smith. During his first season's work Prodgers had climbed up to the egg-shaped stone, a huge chunk of rock fifteen feet high and fourteen feet in diameter. He had blown it to pieces with dynamite and then excavated for twelve feet. Later he wrote that he found an opening between two rocks through which he pushed a bamboo pole for a distance of twelve feet. Evil-smelling gas poured out and he was compelled to scramble out in a hurry. Like Sanders, he believed that the document was inaccurate.

Smith, who had partnered Prodgers in 1907, returned to the site in 1927 to drive a fifty-foot tunnel into the eastern side of the Cavallo Cunca, with several galleries branching off. He eventually struck the shaft of an old Jesuit mine, choked with fallen rock. He used dynamite, which was a great mistake for after the blast there was a prolonged rumbling sound which continued for nearly an hour, caused by a massive slide of rock in the depths below. This landslide alone may indicate that the treasure may never be recovered if by chance Smith had actually been above the treasure chamber. It is a fact, though, that the whole hillside is honeycombed with natural caverns, many more than those hewn out by the Jesuits.

Grimly, Smith started a new tunnel further down the hill-side hoping to connect with the old shaft. Some measure of his determination may be gained from the fact that this tunnel, which he cut single-handed, is more than a hundred yards long and has a number of side galleries. He failed however, to link up with the Jesuit shaft. When Sanders explored Smith's workings he found them walled up, and freeing them, exposed the network of galleries, each one of which came to a dead end.

Sanders may have been right in his conviction that the treasure was under the Square Stone Heap for he learned that in 1927 a party of Turks or Armenians had brought a metal detecting device to Plazuela. They had no results at all until they reached the Square Stone Heap, where the needle suddenly pointed downwards at the exact spot at which Sanders' expedition had been working.

To this date, there have been no further attempts to unearth the treasure at Plazuela and it is almost certain that it still remains to be found, in spite of the many efforts of the adventurers who have tried their luck through the years. The Cavallo Cunca, the hill which contains the treasure, is, according to the document, a steep hill, nearly a thousand feet in height, situated on the bank of the River Sacambaya opposite the ruins of the old monastery. Careful thought will have to be given to the contents of the document in order to determine its true meaning from the several translations that have been published over the intervening years.

The Mysterious Treasure
of Rennes le Château

One of the most mysterious and cryptic stories of hidden riches is centred around the church at Rennes le Château, an ancient settlement in the mountainous country of the south of France, located just a mile from the village of Rennes les Bains and thirty miles south of Carcassonne in the Aude Department. In centuries past Rennes le Château was known as Aereda (Rhedae), and it was one of the last strongholds of the Visigoths, a Germanic tribe whose kingdom once spread right across southern France and into Spain. In AD 501, this kingdom – the kingdom of Toulouse – was attacked and overthrown by the Franks. Aereda was abandoned and eventually fell into dilapidation. Later, it was rebuilt and renamed Rennes le Château, and soon a small village grew up around the church.

The first inkling of the existence of a buried hoard came early in the 1800s when a shepherd, while chasing one of his straying flock, chanced upon the hillside entrance to a cave or vault. Following the tunnel in search of his errant lamb, he found himself in a crypt which he later described as being full of skeletons and coffers. The coffers, he soon discovered, were full of gold coin and he became scared and left, but not until he had crammed his pockets with as many coins as he could carry. The rest of the villagers soon learned of his good fortune and demanded to know where the entrance to the vault was. When the shepherd refused to show them, they ridiculed his story, accused him of theft and summarily executed him.

Thus the treasure continued to lie undisturbed and, in 1885, the little church of Rennes le Château received a new curate, whose name was Beranger Saunière. On his arrival in the tiny village, he was taken in and cared for by the Denarnaud family. Soon, however, he realized their extreme poverty and that his presence exacerbated the overcrowded conditions in which, like many peasants, they lived. In order to improve their lot he asked for, and obtained, church permission for them to move into the presbytery – an act of kindness that may have been also motivated by the development of an attraction between himself and the Denarnauds' teenage daughter, Marie. He arranged for Marie to assist him in the running of the church and they became constant companions.

Early in the year 1891 Beranger managed to obtain a grant to do some restoration work to the church, especially the altar and the roof, and for this task he employed the services of a stonemason named Babon, from the nearby town of Couiza. During the course of his work, Babon discovered that the ancient altar pillars were hollow and, inside one of them, found four or five wooden rolls sealed with wax. Carefully Beranger opened one and saw that it contained a strange parchment inscribed with a mixture of French and Latin, appearing at first glance to be a passage from one of the Gospels. He took the rolls away and began a thorough perusal of all the parchments.

News of this find soon reached the ears of the Mayor, who sought out the priest and requested details. Knowing full well that the Mayor would be unable to read the documents, Beranger willingly showed them to him, informing him that they were worthless papers relating to the Revolution. This seemed to satisfy the Mayor's curiosity and the matter appeared to be settled – except that Beranger suddenly ordered a cessation of the restoration work.

In February 1892 the priest made a trip to Paris where he deposited some of the documents with skilled church paleographers. While he waited for the results, he was not idle. He went the social rounds and made the acquaintance of the world-famous opera singer Emma Calvé, friend of the composer Claude Debussy, and formed a relationship that was to continue long after his return to his remote hilltop village. It is not known if Beranger submitted all the documents that he found to the paleographers; probably he did not, for what he learned from those he did have examined sent him hurrying to the Louvre to buy a copy of a painting by Poussin, the 'Shepherds of Arcadia'. At any rate, by the time of his return to Rennes le Château he had acquired enough information to convince him that there was a treasure concealed somewhere underneath his church. He confided the secret to Marie and together they set out to unravel the mystery.

It seems that one of the parchments contained measurements in fathoms, starting at the altar and, according to Beranger's calculations, arriving at a terminal point known as the 'castle', now merely a piece of waste ground. The documents also directed attention to a certain tomb in the churchyard – the tomb of Marie de Nègre dans de Blanchefort. The gravestone and the headstone of this tomb were carved with strange inscriptions. By deciphering these and using the result in conjunction with the information in the parchments, Marie and Beranger were prompted to dig at a certain spot. There they succeeded in locating the entrance to the long-lost treasure vault.

It is thought that Beranger disposed of some pieces of the treasure by selling them in Spain, Switzerland and Germany; certainly he soon amassed a considerable fortune. Whereas his account book for 1890 showed him to be almost penniless, by 1893 he was proceeding with the restoration work on a far more lavish scale, and paying for this out of his own pocket. He had the presbytery repaired and a new wall built around the churchyard. A summer house was constructed in a rock garden with playing fountains, and he ordered the three-mile cart track leading to the village to be made up into a good modern highway. Marie kept open house for all the neighbouring gentry and, meanwhile, Beranger purchased houses and land, the deeds of which he put in her name. The living was high and the sudden acquisition of untold wealth may have gone slightly to his head, but he was shrewd enough to obliterate all obvious clues to the location of the vault, for there was still a great deal of the treasure left. He was at great pains to scrape away the strange inscriptions on the grave and headstone.

Using this last action as an excuse, the Mayor called on Beranger to complain at what he considered to be the unjustified defacing of the tomb, and to demand an explanation of the priest's sudden affluence. Beranger sat him down at a table loaded with delicious foods and wine, telling him that a relative had died and left him a rich legacy. Afterwards he gave the Mayor a handsome gift of money and sent him on his way. The Mayor accepted the explanation and the money, but he frequently returned for the same reasons and the same price.

News of Beranger's extravagance eventually reached the ears of the Bishop of Carcassonne, who decided to pay a personal visit to Rennes le Château. He was given the same explanation and treated in the same way.

Beranger the Benevolent continued to expand his mode of living. In 1897 he commissioned the building of a villa with ramparts and a tower, at an estimated cost of one million francs. He installed a library in the tower and took up residence in luxurious style. During this time the old Bishop of Carcassonne retired and his successor, Monsignor de Beauséjour, immediately demanded a fuller explanation of the source of Beranger's wealth. When the priest hedged, the Bishop had him summoned before the court of Rome and finally suspended from office. A new priest was nominated for Rennes le Château, but Beranger declined to take the slightest notice of either the Bishop or the new priest. He continued to say Mass at the church, and the villagers stood by him until the Bishop eventually gave up and washed his hands of the whole affair.

Beranger lived high, wide and handsome, but never forgot the people who had remained devoted to him. In January 1917 he signed an order to pay for water to be laid on for the entire village, the cost of which amounted to eight million francs. He was not to see this work carried out, however, for it seemed that he was reaping what may have been the rewards of his bonanza. He was critically ill with cirrhosis of the liver and on 22 January he died, leaving Marie the sole beneficiary of his fabulous find.

With Beranger gone, Marie was the only person who knew the secret of the vault's location but, as she was provided with more than enough money to last the rest of her life, it is unlikely that she ever visited the hidden chamber again. In fact, for years she shut herself away – a recluse. This changed in 1946, when a M. Corbu and his wife came to live with her.

They became firm friends and eventually Marie told them the whole story. In her last days Marie bequeathed the house to Corbu and told him not to worry about the future, that he would have more money than he would know what to do with. However she held back exact information on the location of the crypt, saying that it was her intention to impart this last secret just before she died. But on 18 January 1953, Marie suffered some sort of stroke. By then she was in her eighties and she went into a coma from which she never regained consciousness. Thus she died without passing on the secret and, to this day, the remainder of the treasure has not been rediscovered, although research in recent years has shown that there is no shortage of clues.

Of the parchments that Saunière found, the first contains a hidden message that is relatively easy to find. The text of the document is arranged on the page in rather an odd manner and quite the most obvious are the letters which are raised higher than the rest. Reading them off in sequence, they say 'This treasure belongs to Dagobert II, King, and to Sion, and he is here dead.'

The second parchment is far from easy and, in fact, it contains the main message, but this message is enciphered by the use of a unique and most complex system that must have taken months of work. The paleographers in Paris found that a key was required to read the message, and this key turned out to be hidden in the inscriptions that Beranger so carefully scraped off the head- and gravestone in his churchyard. Did he but know it, his efforts were wasted, for the inscription had been copied some years before and preserved in a little booklet. As in the case of the first parchment, the key was easy to find. The headstone inscription contained obvious mistakes in almost every line and by gathering these together – eight in all – the key phrase was arrived at: 'mort épée'.

In their examination of the second parchment, the paleographers found that it consisted of a Gospel text into which 140 extra letters had been inserted. From these the middle twelve, which stood out above the rest, had to be rejected, and the remaining 128 letters were laid out in one of the standard cipher systems – that known as the Vigenère – and the key

phrase 'mort épée' applied. But this decipherment only
produced another batch of meaningless letters, and the paleographers found that the next step required them to shift the
whole text one place forward in the alphabet. For H they
wrote I, for Q they wrote R, and so on. Finding the result a
new but meaningless jumble, they realized that a new key
was now needed. And this proved to be the entire text of the
headstone, plus two letters from the gravestone. Using the
Vigenère system again, but applying the key backwards and
ending with the two extra letters, yet another series of letters
resulted – and still meaningless. Now it became necessary to
shift the text once more, this time two places in the alphabet.
But still the result was meaningless, and the next step required
to solve this amazing cipher was extraordinary.

The paelographers found that they had to take this fourth
set of jumbled letters and divide them into two groups of
sixty-four each. Taking the first group, they laid them out on
a chessboard. Then, after selecting the correct starting square,
they made the only sequence of Knight moves possible that
will cover the entire board using each square only once. The
second group of sixty-four were applied in the same way but
read off with the moves reversed, mirror fashion. And at last the
final message emerged. The most amazing confirmation of the
validity of the deciphered message was that it was found to be a
perfect anagram of the text of the headstone which provided
the key. The message reads:

SHEPHERDESS NO TEMPTATION TO WHICH POUSSIN
TENIERS HOLD THE KEY   PEACE 681   BY THE CROSS OF
THIS HORSE OF GOD I COMPLETE THIS DAEMON GUARD-
IAN AT MIDDAY BLUE APPLES.

Even today, much of this message still cannot be explained,
but it does indicate why Beranger purchased the copy of
Poussin's 'Shepherds of Arcadia'. It is the first clue in the
deciphered message. The canvas depicts a shepherdess in the
company of three shepherds, contemplating a tomb in a
pastoral landscape. On the tomb are inscribed the words
Et in Arcadia ego (I, too, have lived in Arcady). This quotation is a direct link to the gravestone whose inscription was

obliterated by Saunière. That too was inscribed with the same quotation, but slightly disguised by employing the use of Greek letters in a Latin text.

Not far from the churchyard at Rennes le Château is a strange-looking structure. It is the tomb depicted in Poussin's painting – even the round stone on which, in the picture, the shepherd rests his foot, is still in place. Art historians have always assumed that the tomb and the landscape were a product of Poussin's imagination, but except for a small detail, the match is precise with the view at Rennes le Château. Nearby is the hill on top of which are the ruins of Blanchefort and it is accurately reproduced in the painting. If you visit the tomb and stand where the painter would have stood you will see, on the horizon to the right, a small hill exactly placed by Poussin. It is the hill of Rennes le Château. The only detail of the scene that does not match in the painting is a mountain slope that rises. In the picture it falls. Could it be that Poussin actually visited Rennes le Château to paint this picture? Was he in possession of the secret of the treasure location? The writer Henry Lincoln has been on the trail of this hoard for some time now, and in the course of his research has unearthed a letter which may be a valuable clue. It is addressed to Nicolas Fouquet, Superintendent of Finance to the court of Louis XIV, and sent to him by his brother who had just visited Poussin in Rome. Dated 17 April 1656, it says:

He and I discussed certain things which I shall with ease be able to explain to you in detail. Things which will give you, through Monsieur Poussin, advantages which even kings will have great pains to draw from him and which, according to him, it is possible that nobody else will rediscover in the centuries to come, and what is more, these are things so difficult to discover that nothing now on this earth can prove a better fortune, or be its equal.

It does appear that Poussin knew something, and it is a fact that, of all his works, 'Shepherds of Arcadia' was the one which was sculpted on his tomb when he died in 1665.

Intrigued by the connection that Poussin may have had with the treasure, Lincoln went to the Louvre and requested that the famous painting be X-rayed. In particular he was interested in the mountain slope that falls in the picture instead of rising, and he hoped that X-rays would reveal that Poussin did at first paint in the slope, but later altered it to a line of cloud. In this he was disappointed, for the X-rays showed no hidden line under the surface paint. But then a minute detail came to light in another part of the picture, a detail so small that only X-rays could have shown it up. The line of a shepherd's staff in the foreground was cut off by the line of the tomb, indicating that the staff must have been painted first. Why? One would expect Poussin would have painted the landscape first and then added the foreground figures, not the other way round. Then it was further revealed that the line of the shepherd's arm divides the staff exactly in two – and this occurs on another staff in the picture. This information prompted Lincoln to have the picture analysed by Professor Cornford of the Royal College of Art, who found that the geometry of the painting contained the figure of a regular pentagon. This was extremely surprising because this system had been discarded centuries before Poussin's time. Why had he resurrected it?

Continuing the analysis, Professor Cornford found that the pentagon was not contained in the area of the painting, but was larger and governed its form from without. This could only result from Poussin's selecting a precise ratio of height and width for his canvas. When the opposite points of the pentagon were joined geometrically, the result was a pentacle – the five pointed star – and the pivotal centre of this star was on the head of the shepherdess. Lincoln had found that a pentacle appeared on some of Saunière's parchments, but had not realized their significance until the revelation of the occult star in the painting. The meaning is clear. It is the first word of the deciphered message, SHEPHERDESS.

The meaning of the next two words, NO TEMPTATION, was discovered by Lincoln when he followed the trail to Shugborough Hall in Staffordshire. In the house was a painting by Poussin of 'Shepherds of Arcadia' – not a copy of the Louvre painting, but another version which Poussin painted some years earlier. With it was a copy of a painting by Teniers. This artist painted many versions of the temptation of St Anthony but

the copy in Shugborough Hall is that of St Anthony and
St Jerome – the only St Anthony theme where he is not being
tempted – and there is a shepherdess in the background of the
picture, too. Thus NO TEMPTATION.

Lincoln found one other highly interesting link at Shugborough Hall. In the grounds there is another stone upon
which is sculpted the Shepherds of Arcadia, only this time the
picture is reversed – mirror fashion. Underneath there is a
cipher which no one has so far broken. It reads 'OUOSVAVV'.
This mysterious monument was erected sometime in the
eighteenth century, and no one seems to know exactly why. The
Hall itself was begun in 1693 and enlarged in 1748. Since 1720
it has been the home of the Anson family, but in the 1960s
became National Trust property.

Returning to the parchments, you may remember that the
first message reads 'This treasure belongs to Dagobert II,
King, and to Sion, and he is here dead.' Continuing his investigations, Lincoln found that King Dagobert II was one of
the last kings of the Merovingian dynasty in France, a dynasty
which reigned over the kingdom of the Franks. This is plain
enough, but the odd factor in the message is the word 'Sion',
meaning Zion or Jerusalem. What connection could there
possibly be? The legendary treasure of Jerusalem, the treasure
of King Solomon's Temple, was carried off by the Romans
when they sacked the city in AD 70. There is a painting by
Poussin of this atrocity. In the year AD 410, Rome in its turn
was sacked by the Visigoths, who carried off the treasure of
Jerusalem and may possibly have brought it back to their
kingdom of Toulouse. I have mentioned that Aereda was one
of their strongholds and it is certain that they kept a large part
of their spoils of war at Carcassonne. In AD 507 the Visigoths
had been overthrown by the Franks – over whom Dagobert
had reigned. It is possible that the treasure of Rennes le
Château is the lost treasure of Jerusalem?

The word 'Sion' appears more than once in the parchments.
At one point it is shown simply reversed, and in another place
it appears, owing to a haphazard placement of words, as the
last letters of four consecutive lines. But before the premise
that it is a direct reference to Jerusalem can be accepted, one

other factor has to be considered. In his many researches Lincoln found several references to a Priory of Sion, and part of the key to decipherment of the message lay in the letters 'P.S.' engraved on the gravestone. What, then, is the Priory of Sion?

Lincoln found the answer to this in a little booklet in the Bibliothèque Nationale, Paris. It contains details of family trees which attempt to establish a line of descent from King Dagobert II. But on another page there appears a list of names of people who have, so the booklet claims, been the alleged Grand Masters of the Priory of Sion – an order which was founded by the Knights Templar.

It is at this point that the investigation of Beranger's lucky find takes a highly interesting turn, for beneath the 'Knight Templar' heading of the list appear in smaller print the words 'Rosie Crois'. And one of the names on the list is that of Nicolas Flamel, one of the most famous alchemists of the Middle Ages. Other equally fascinating names are on that list: Leonardo da Vinci, Isaac Newton, Victor Hugo, Claude Debussy and Jean Cocteau. On another page of the booklet there is a strange coat of arms under which there is the motto *'Et in Arcadia ego'*. The 'Rosie Crois' (or Rosy Cross) is the emblem of the Rosicrucians, and so we can see that an unusual connection is being formed between the treasure, the Rosicrucians and alchemy.

Although there are some Orders of the Rosicrucians that are quite open, the true Order is highly secret – the most secret of secret societies. Writing almost one hundred years ago, Madame Blavatsky said: 'No one could ever lay hands on the Rosicrucians, and notwithstanding the alleged discoveries of "secret chambers", vellums called "T", and of fossil knights with ever-burning lamps, this ancient association and its true aims are to this day a mystery.'

It is still not known for sure how the Order first came into existence, but some claim that it was founded by the alchemist Paracelsus. Others claim that the true origin is that which is described in the manuscript called the *Fama Fraternitatis*, published in 1614. It describes how one Christian Rozenkreuz (from whom the Order took its name) journeyed to the East where he was given the Wisdom of the Ancients. On his return to Germany he imparted this knowledge to eight other initiates, who then separated, each going to another country to found different branches of the Order.

Another derivation of the name is thought to come from the Latin words '*Ros*' – meaning 'dew' and referring to the Dew of May, regarded by the alchemists as the Universal Solvent – and '*crux*', meaning 'cross' and identified with light because the cross contains various presentations of the three capital letters of the word '*lux*', meaning 'light'.

In any case, the link between the Rosicrucians and alchemy is conclusive. Paracelsus, Nicolas Flamel, Elias Ashmole, the Count St Germain, Robert Fludd, Thomas Vaughn and van Helmont – to name only a few – were all Rosicrucians in possession of the higher knowledge of alchemy. But is there a link between alchemy and Rennes le Château?

In one of the parchments found by Saunière, there is yet another hidden phrase. Picked out quite easily in letters that are smaller than the rest of the text, are the words '*Rex Mundi*' ('King of the Earth'). Of course, this phrase could be just another indication that there is a king buried with the treasure – a king in the earth – but *Rex Mundi* is also an epithet applied to the devil, and, strangely enough, there is a devil at Rennes le Château.

With the riches available to him Beranger made some remarkable alterations to the little church there. Over the door, he had carved an inscription in Latin. Translated, it reads 'This place is terrible'. The interior of the church is a mass of detailed, flamboyant decoration. Curious decorations which border on bad taste – certainly not what one would expect to find in the quiet sanctity of a small village church. On a scene depicting Christ giving succour to the afflicted there is portrayed a money bag. Just inside the door stands a hideous statue of the devil, mounted above a small water trough, and nearby are other statues, painted angels with glassy, empty-looking eyes. On the walls are salamanders, the alchemists' symbol of fire. Did Saunière attempt to portray the four elements of alchemy? Air in the spirit of the angels, Water in the trough, Fire in the salamanders, and Earth, *Rex Mundi*, the devil? If so, it points to a drastic change of religious belief by the priest. It is a fact that on his deathbed Saunière made a confession that profoundly shocked the priest who heard it – and what would shock a priest more than an admission of what amounts to devil-worship?

In a recent television programme Henry Lincoln brought many of these facts to light and made some interesting connections with the Albigenses, who worshipped *Rex Mundi*. This long-gone heresy denied Christ as part of their religion, an accusation that was also levelled at the Templars. Both these obscure faiths seem to be base offshoots of a higher knowledge that has been preserved from remote antiquity – and this, of course, brings us back to the true Rosicrucians.

It is difficult to place a date on the founding of the Priory of Sion for, although the pillar in which the documents were found is from the time of King Dagobert, the cipher which was employed in the parchments is of much later date. Though the cipher used is now known as the Vigenère system, the alphabet square used in this system was first invented by Johannes Trithemus, a Benedictine monk – and an alchemist – whose book on cryptology was published in 1518. An advance on this method was the introduction of a key word or phrase by a certain Giovan Batista Belaso. His book was published in 1553. Blaise de Vigenère took it one step further and invented the constantly changing key, which he called the auto-key. Vigenère's work on this was published in 1586, and now the system is universally called after him. It may be noted that Vigenère was also an alchemist and that Poussin regularly referred to his works when composing a theme to paint.

Poussin's second version – the Louvre version – of the 'Shepherds of Arcadia' was painted in the mid-1650s, and we have seen that there is the evidence of Fouquet's letter to indicate that he knew about the treasure in 1656. This seems to prove that the encipherment of the parchments took place sometime between about 1550 and about 1650, that the Priory of Sion was then in existence and that its members had knowledge of the immense cache. While not an alchemist himself, Poussin had a circle of extremely learned friends, and it is known that he had a strong tendency towards Stoicism.

If the Rosicrucians held the secret of the treasure of Rennes le Château in, say, 1600 why was it being saved? To what use would this hoard eventually be put? When Saunière happened upon the secret did he become a member of the Priory of Sion? He certainly received many distinguished visitors during the time he held sway in the ancient *château*. Was the long-kept secret imparted to him? The building in which he lived is known as the Tower of Alchemy. Who ordered and designed the monument at Shugborough Hall, and what is the meaning of the cipher carved on it?

Much has yet to be learned regarding this mysterious treasure cache. The full significance of the Teniers painting has yet to be discovered, as has the meaning of the last line of the deciphered message, PEACE 681 BY THE CROSS OF THIS HORSE OF GOD I COMPLETE THIS DAEMON GUARDIAN AT MIDDAY BLUE APPLES. Here I can make one small but not very helpful suggestion. It is usually held that King Dagobert II was assassinated in AD 679, but this may not be correct. May not the phrase PEACE 681 indicate the true date of his interment with the treasure? The dates are close.

Henry Lincoln has offered the controversial opinion that the source of Beranger's wealth came, not from a buried cache of gold, but from resources supplied by members of the Priory of Sion. It was still in existence in his time – remember that Claude Debussy's name was on the list of Grand Masters. This is certainly possible, if Saunière had stumbled on something of infinite value to the members of the Order – something other than treasure. However, I cannot agree with this idea. Let it be noted that, for all his affluence, Beranger clung tenaciously to his little hilltop *château*, and yet he showed no dislike for the better things that money could buy. Marie, in her last days, averred that there was still a tremendous amount of wealth left in the vault, and there was no reason for her not to tell the truth.

Without doubt Beranger went to great pains to conceal the entrance to the cache, but it would be contrary to human nature for him to have concealed it beyond the bounds of human recovery.

The Lost Dutchman Mine

In the turbulent years when the great south-western territories of the United States were overrun and exploited by white settlers from the east, one of the richest prizes was the discovery of abundant mineral deposits. Lead, copper, silver and gold were found in plenty across the wide area that is now New Mexico, Arizona and California. The most well known is the strike which resulted in the California Gold Rush of 1849, and the sudden surge of publicity which followed tended to overshadow the other notable finds that were being made all over the rest of the south-west area.

Apart from the many syndicated mining companies that were formed to exploit this mineral treasure, the whole of the territory was crawling with itinerant prospectors, each on the trail of his own personal bonanza. They defied the hazards of the waterless deserts, some unsuccessfully, as many bleached bones have testified, and they climbed into the unmapped canyons of the rugged hills to face the threat of death from the Indians, who not surprisingly resented the increasing hordes of white men that were invading their lands.

The lawless and haphazard way in which the lone prospectors worked combined with the severe hardships they endured in tracking over the ruthless terrain to give birth to the myriad of 'lost mine' stories that have attracted treasure hunters ever since.

The best known of these sagas is the legend of the Lost Dutchman Mine, in Arizona. This fabulous pocket of rich ore is situated somewhere in the Superstition Mountains, about forty miles east of the town of Phoenix. To attempt to reach the truth about the Dutchman legend it is necessary to delve into a little of the area's history.

The earliest record of prospecting in what is now the State of Arizona appears in a document describing an expedition led by one Antonio de Espejo, a wealthy mining engineer from Spain. Espejo stated that after he had taken a circuitous route north through New Mexico, and then west into Arizona, he found silver ore at a place now called Bill Williams' Fork, west of Prescott. That was in the year 1582.

Although the area which constitutes these two states was at that time the undisputed home of the Red Indian, the Spanish adventurers from the south indulged in sporadic expeditions and eventually claimed the territory as part of the huge State of Sonora. Evidence is conflicting but it is generally assumed today that the Jesuit priests, who were working numerous rich mines in the Sierra Madre Mountains of Mexico, extended their operations to include southern Arizona, until the Apaches massacred them. The Superstition Mountains were the stronghold of the warlike Apache tribe, under their leader Geronimo, until 1885 when US troops chased them to their last retreat high up in the Sierra Madres.

The Dutchman Mine was probably discovered sometime in the mid-1800s by one of the Mexican expeditions, either members of, or financed by, the family of Enrico Peralta. This family extracted the mineral wealth from the mine at intervals up until 1864, when Enrico Peralta's party was set upon by the Indians. In a three-day battle the vicious Apache warriors slaughtered every one of the mining party. Evidence of this battle came to light in later years, and provided the first substantial clues to the history of the elusive bonanza but from this point, the facts relating to the mine and the central characters are clouded by a welter of fiction. What are considered most likely to be the true facts are in the story that follows, although I hasten to say that only some of them are documented.

Jacob Waltz and his friend and namesake, Jacob Weiser, both of German origin, rescued a Mexican from a brawl in a little town in Sonora. The Mexican, whose name was Don

Miguel Peralta, was grateful, took his rescuers to his home and, within a few days, was pouring out his own misfortunes to the two Americans. He was the heir of Enrico Peralta and, he explained, ever since Enrico had been slain by the Indians, the family had been afraid to go back into the mountains where the gold mine was. As a result the Peralta family fortune had dwindled considerably but since the two Americans seemed to be both resourceful and without fear, Peralta saw a chance to re-establish the missing wealth.

He explained that each family expedition to the mine had cached part of the extracted gold in a place nearby, so as to enable smaller parties to collect it quickly should the need arise. Would Waltz and Weiser accompany him on a quick trip into the hills to pick up the gold under the very nose of the Apache? The two Americans were quite willing to go and the trip was completely successful, realizing a haul of about 60000 dollars. According to their agreement, Peralta took half, while Waltz and Weiser were given a quarter each. And in return for their services, Peralta is said to have insisted that the Americans take the title deeds of the mine for themselves. Whether this was true will never be known, but it is a fact that both Waltz and Weiser each told the same story, at a time when each believed the other to be dead. After this first visit to the mine, which occurred in 1871, Weiser apparently had in his possession a map showing the position of the mine.

In about 1879 Waltz and Weiser decided to return and take out some more of the gold ore. Guided by the map, they reached the spot, only to find that two Mexican peons had stumbled on the secret and were poaching their gold. The two Americans shot the Mexicans and disposed of their bodies in a nearby canyon. Then they set to work digging out the gold. But disaster struck. Returning to their camp one day, Waltz found his partner gone. On the ground lay his bloodstained shirt and tools. Indian arrows told the grim story – he had been murdered by the Indians. Waltz dropped everything and got out of the mountains as fast as he could. Taking all the gold he could carry, he settled down in the nearby town of Phoenix, where he lived until 1891.

But here the tale takes a strange turn for, contrary to Waltz's assumption, his friend Weiser had not been killed. Although severely wounded, he had managed to make his escape and eventually reached the home of a Dr John Walker, to whom he told the whole story before he died. He made no mention of his partner, probably assuming that the Apaches had killed Waltz, and he bequeathed the map to Walker. Walker made no attempt to locate the mine and, on his death in 1890, the map disappeared. He had, however, allowed the editor of a local newspaper to make a copy of it but this was destroyed by the latter's wife who feared that he might meet his death searching for the mine.

Now, it seemed, Waltz was the only one who knew the location of the mine but in 1880 two young men stumbled upon it by accident. The names of these two have not survived, but it is thought they were ex-soldiers. They arrived in the small town of Pinal one day, with their saddlebags bursting with gold ore of unusual purity. Asked where they had found it by a local mine manager, they explained that they had chanced upon a mine in the Superstition Mountains, a funnel-shaped opening in the rocks which led to a rich seam. They had hacked out all the gold they could carry and ridden on to Pinal. Questioned if they could find their way back, they explained that, as they had been taught in the army to note landmarks in reverse, they could easily do so. They indicated that the mine was near a sharp pinnacle of rock.

Encouraged by the mine manager, they set off to ride the twenty-five miles back to the canyon, but not before the news of the strike had spread all over town. The two young soldiers were never seen alive again. Ten days later they were found by a rescue party. Both had been shot dead and stripped naked after the Apache fashion, but it was soon discovered that they had not been shot by Indians. The bullets recovered from the bodies were found to be of a US army pattern. Suspicion fell on a local man, previously poor and now suddenly rich, but nothing could be proved and the man left the district. Later stories attribute the slaying of these two men to Waltz, but at that time he was supposed to be living in Phoenix, although his reputation was unsavoury enough to make him a likely suspect.

By now the story of the mine was becoming widely known

and was erroneously called the Dutchman Mine after Waltz. A number of people claim to have found it, one of whom was a man named Joe Deering. He is reputed to have said, 'You have to go through a hole,' meaning, it was assumed, that the mine could be reached through a cave or cleft in the rocks but soon after his discovery and before he fully explained the location of his discovery, he died in an accident at another mine where he worked.

It is also thought that the Apaches finally took a hand in concealing the mine forever. According to a story told later by an Indian named Apache Jack, who was only a boy at the time, the squaws were set to work during the winter periods of 1881 and 1882 and the pit was entirely filled in, with all traces of it obliterated.

In 1890 Waltz left his home in Phoenix and went off into the Superstitions, returning two days later with a sack of rich ore worth about 1500 dollars. He told friends that this came from a cache which had been deposited by himself and Weiser. Waltz died in 1891 and on his deathbed related the story of his early visits to the mine. He tried to give directions by which the mine could be found, but his listeners either failed to understand his directions or deliberately kept the details to themselves. Since none of them ever found the mine, the story they told in later years may have been the truth.

'The mine,' stated Waltz, 'is situated in very rough country, so rough that you could be right in the mine without seeing it.' He described the ore as being very rich and easy to take out of the rock. Nuggets of gold simply fell out when he and Weiser tapped the rock with their hammers. The mine was supposed to contain an eighteen-inch vein of rose-coloured quartz, liberally impregnated with gold nuggets, plus a second vein of hematite quartz, which was about one-third gold.

The mine itself was in the shape of a funnel with the large end up. Shelves had been cut in the wall so that the miners could use them to help in carrying the loads up from the bottom. Don Enrico Peralta had cut a tunnel through the hillside into the bottom of the pit to make extraction easier – a fact that tallies with the statement made by the unfortunate Deering.

The witnesses present at Waltz's death were Dick Holmes, Julia Thomas and a local baker, Reinhart Petrash. According to a story later told by Holmes, Waltz confessed to the killing of a nephew. Apparently Waltz had decided that he would share the mine with his family and sent word for his nephew Julius to come out from Germany. Julius arrived and shared the secret of the mine, but showed signs of a loose tongue while in his cups. Waltz was not a man to take chances and disposed of him at the first opportunity, in the same way that he got rid of the Mexicans. Holmes later claimed to have found Julius's skull.

Petrash made several attempts to find the mine, all of them unsuccessful. He stated that Waltz told him that 'The mine is near the hideout cave. One mile from the cave, there is a rock with a natural face looking east. To the south is Weaver's Needle. Follow the right of two canyons, but not far. The mine faces west.' Weaver's Needle is a pinnacle of rock long associated with the Lost Dutchman Mine that in earlier times was aptly called 'El Sombrero' by the Mexicans.

In the area of this natural monument evidence was found that indicated that a large party of Mexicans had camped there and worked. A pile of one hundred sandals was discovered in the cleft of a rock, while firebeds and deeply worn trails proved that a large number of men and animals had visited the spot periodically. A mass of tree stumps of a variety not suitable for burning, probably ironwood, suggested that the trees had been felled for pit props, and in 1912 two prospectors found gold ingots strewn in the grass at the exact site of the traditional last stand of Enrico Peralta's party. Nearby in the mountains were found the crumbling bones of many mules, probably killed for food by the Apache.

With the death of Waltz the stories of the mine grew, and attempts to find the gold knew no bounds. In 1895 a man named James Addison Reavis was convicted of forging a series of documents showing, falsely, a Land Grant to a (mythical) Don Miguel Peralta. Reavis travelled to Mexico and even to Spain in order to insert his forgeries into the ancient registers. Generations of imaginary ancestors were created for 'Don Miguel', and Reavis himself married a Mexican girl whom he 'proved' was the last descendant of the Peralta family, the inheritor of ten million acres of land in Arizona and heiress to twenty-five million dollars. Reavis' imposture and the mythical nature of his Peralta Land Grant was exposed in 1947 by Lawrence Buddington Kelland of the *Saturday Evening Post*.

In the years following the demise of Jacob Waltz, some twenty treasure hunters lost their lives, either by accident or by murder. In 1928, two deer hunters in the Superstitions reported that an unknown person had rolled huge boulders down on them. Dick Holmes, after many unsuccessful attempts to locate the mine, died in 1930.

In June 1931 sixty-six-year-old Adolph Ruth somehow got hold of a copy of a map which had belonged to the Peralta family. He recognized that it was a guide to the Lost Dutchman Mine and determined to find it. He went into the mountain and never came out. Six months later, a party of archaeologists discovered Adolph Ruth's skull with a bullet hole in the left temple, with the rest of the body nearby. In the pocket of what was left of his jacket was a piece of paper on which was scrawled some directions, ending 'about 200 feet across from cave. *Veni, vidi, vici.*' The map, however, was gone.

Two men from Phoenix, Blaine and Schweiger, were hiking in the mountains in 1932 when they were shot at by an unknown rifleman. The hidden marksman kept them pinned behind a boulder until nightfall when they were able to make their escape. In 1943 the last link with Waltz's death was broken when Reinhart Petrash died. He had not been able to find the mine.

To date, the mine has not been found although the inhospitable region has claimed a dozen victims. Local authorities do not forbid expeditions into the wild regions of the Superstitions, but they do their best to dissuade all but the most experienced from trying. Too many people have failed to come back.

What, in fact, did happen to the Dutchman Mine? Its existence is hardly in any doubt, but since 1879, when Waltz and Weiser were attacked while working the mine, no one has seen it and returned to tell. It may be remembered that, one year before his death, Waltz went into the Superstitions and returned with a sack of ore. One of the last statements attributed to Waltz is that he covered up the mine on that occasion by putting some ironwood logs over the pit and shovelling rocks on top of the logs. Maybe the story told by Apache Jack was true, and the Indians did fill in the pit in 1882. In that case Waltz could have retrieved his sack of ore from a known cache, marked the location of the buried mine and returned but it has been said by one of the three witnesses at Waltz's death that he stated that he never went near the mine after 1879.

The fact remains that the mine is there, somewhere near Weaver's Needle. The story still attracts many seekers, some of whom seem to lose their sense of proportion completely once they are in the location. As late as June 1959 Stanley Fernandez, who had come all the way from Hawaii to search, was murdered in the Superstitions by his partner, Benjamin Ferreira – because he refused to dig!

Should you decide to go and look for it – no law will stop you – choose the winter months. It will be cold, but it seldom gets dangerously cold and, should your water supplies give out, you will have a good chance of finding water from a spring. In the summer months you will very likely die of thirst. If you buy a map, get a Government Survey edition and also make your own map as you go in – a map of where you have been, with all available landmarks and trails marked. Probably you will be offered a 'treasure' map – their sale is a thriving industry over there with all the mapmakers eagerly awaiting the arrival of the next tenderfoot – but don't waste your money on it. Wear strong shoes with thick soles, take a snakebite kit, carry a good rifle and – most important – don't go alone!

The Lost Mines of the Muribeca

In the early 1500s a Portuguese mariner, Diego Alvarez, was the sole survivor of a shipwreck off the coast of what is now San Salvador, Brazil. As a virtual castaway, he lived for many years among the Tupimambas, a tribe of local Indians, and eventually married an Indian girl named Paraguassu. In time the spot where Alvarez came ashore grew into a thriving port known as Bahia de São Salvador de todos os Santos – or Bahia for short.

Paraguassu's sister married another Portuguese adventurer and their offspring, Melchoir Dias Moreyra, spent all his life with the Indians, becoming known to them as the Muribeca. He discovered hidden deep in the jungle of the interior, not only a wealth of precious stones and gold, but also an extremely large and rich deposit of silver and, using the Indians as a labour force, he was able to mine large quantities of the rich ore whenever he needed. Before he died, he revealed to his son, Roberio Dias, the location of the hidden mine.

As the Muribeca's heir, Dias soon grew into one of the wealthiest and most respected landowners in Bahia but he was not satisfied, for he was a commoner by birth and he aspired to a nobler heritage. He evolved a scheme whose success would result in his being invited to join the court of the Portuguese King, Dom Pedro II. It was sometime in the early 1600s when Dias approached the King with an offer to divulge the secret of his vast mines in exchange for the royal title of Marquis das Minas (Marquis of the Mines). His ploy to arouse the greed of the King seemed to be successful. A patent was duly drawn up, sealed and delivered to a commission with instructions to hand it over only after the secret of the mines had been disclosed. But Dias was suspicious. While the expedition into the interior was still a few days away from Bahia, he persuaded the officer commanding the commission to let him break the seal and read the patent. He found that he had been granted no marquisate but merely a military commission as a captain. Incensed at this double dealing, Dias refused to lead the way to the mines, at which he was taken back to Bahia by force and thrown into a prison cell.

Strenuous efforts were made to pry the necessary information out of him during the two years that he was gaoled, but his lips remained sealed and in 1622 he died, taking the secret with him. The only other people who knew where the mines lay were the Indians, and it was well known that, even when subjected to the most vicious tortures, no Indian would talk. Thus the story grew into a legend that became known as the Lost Mines of the Muribeca and for the next hundred and fifty years many treasure hunters defied the rigours of the jungle in an effort to locate the hidden wealth.

One party, comprising a group of Portuguese adventurers, their Negro slaves and some Indian guides, set out in determined mood. For a full ten years no more was heard of them. Then they returned to Bahia with a tale of how they had wandered all that time in the trackless interior before being rewarded by success, and one of the party produced a lengthy and detailed account of what they had found – no less than an ancient and deserted city and, close by, abandoned workings which they identified as the long-lost Muribeca Mines. The document was sent to the Viceroy at Rio de Janeiro who read it, hid it in the archives and said nothing. One can only guess at his reasons and why no reported efforts were subsequently made to return to the mines. It is, however, known for certain that the *Relatório*, as the document is now called, lay forgotten in the old public library in Rio for ninety years until it was brought to light by the historian and archivist Senhor Lagos in 1841.

It is now listed as MSS 512 in the Biblioteca Nacional, Rio de Janeiro. Over the years it has suffered the ravages of the copim, a South American insect with an apparently voracious appetite for paper, and several significant sentences are missing. Recent investigation has revealed that it was written by a João da Silva Guimaroes in 1753. After outlining the story of the Muribeca and naming the Lost Muribeca Mines as his party's objective, the writer goes on to describe how, in the tenth year of their wandering in the jungle, the group came upon an unusually high range of mountains, composed almost entirely of rock crystal. The effects of the sun's rays reflecting on the white crystal and shining through a rain shower excited their admiration and they decided to make camp at the foot of the range.

Game was plentiful and the surrounding terrain was pleasing to the eye after many months of hacking their way through the thick forest. For some days they scouted the lower foothills in and effort to find a pass through the high cordillera, but without success and it looked as if they would be forced to make the huge detour round them. Sheer chance came to the rescue when one of the Negroes, gathering wood for the fire, spotted a white deer and gave chase. As it fled, the deer ran into an almost hidden canyon, and it was here that the Negro discovered an ancient paved roadway leading upwards. His excited shouts brought the others and they set out to climb the road. As the party toiled up through the canyon of rock crystal, they saw that the road had suffered great cracks and fallen boulders, probably the result of past earthquakes. It took them three hours to reach the summit. Beyond lay an open plain and, some three miles distant, they saw, to their great excitement, the grey stone walls of a city.

It speaks much of their caution that they waited two days before sending out an Indian scout to discover who the inhabitants might be. Although a constant watch had been kept, no sign of life – not even smoke from a fire – had been reported. Soon the Indian returned with the news that the city was completely deserted and, filled with curiosity, the whole group went to investigate. Entering the walled city through its main gate, a huge, three-arched construction, they found themselves in a wide street. On each side were large houses, whose façades of sculptured stone were blackened with age. No furniture could be found in the gloomy interior of the huge rooms for it had long since rotted to dust, and their voices echoed from the vaults, heightening their fear.

Making their way into the centre of the city, they came to a road of great length, beside which was a well-laid-out *plaza*. In the centre of the square stood an object of great interest, a tall black basalt column, on top of which was the carved figure of a man, left hand on hip and right arm outstretched. The index finger, they noted, was pointing towards the north pole. At each corner of the square there stood an obelisk, but these were badly damaged. The writer describes at great length some of the larger houses and the carved artwork of the façades, and one of the most interesting points of the manuscript is the inclusion of several unique hieroglyphics which he took the trouble to copy while they were there. These strange characters have baffled the most eminent authorities, for they have not yet been deciphered.

Alongside the *plaza*, the writer continues, they found a swiftly running river, some seventy feet wide and with a depth of almost a hundred feet. It was this river that eventually led them to the mines.

When they had thoroughly explored the dead city, the group set off downstream. After about three days' journeying they came to a waterfall of some magnitude and their progress was halted. Attracted by the strange booming noise of the waterfall, they investigated and on the eastern bank discovered many large pits of incalculable depth. Some of these mysterious holes were covered over by special slabs of stone, into which were carved more of the strange hieroglyphics. Loosely scattered around were a number of silver bars. Had they, at last, found the long-lost Mines of the Muribeca? Although they were unable to get down into the pits, the writer had no doubt that they had.

Senhor Lagos' discovery of the document giving these details sparked off an immediate flare of interest in the mines and a number of people made their way to Rio to pore over the aged document. One, a young canon of a theological college in Bahia named Conego Benigno, firmly believed that he could pinpoint the ancient workings. After careful consideration of the geographical clues given in the *Relatório*, he announced that the lost city and the mines must be in the Serra do Cincora, a range of mountains located some three hundred miles inland from Bahia, and approached the government in the hope of financial backing for a small expedition. Such was his faith, even though the authorities were reluctant to part with a fraction of the sum required, he set out on his own.

Leaving Bahia on 23 December 1841, he journeyed up the Paraguaçu River and into the Una tributary mentioned in the *Relatório*. From there, he struck out into the wild interior with a mule and some pack-horses. Only one month later, he lay desperately ill with fever at a farm on the edge of the jungle. It was a fever which was to stay with him for five months and waste him away to a mere skeleton. His mule had broken its back and one of the horses had died. In the archives – along with the *Relatório* – is to be found his final letter to the government, an impassioned plea for funds. It starkly portrays the young priest's ill-fortune.

But the local stories he had heard served only to increase his conviction that the *Relatório* told the truth. The Paraguaçu and the Una had led him directly to the foot of the Serra do Cincora, which was, as Benigno knew, the highest and most inaccessible mountain range in the province of Bahia, and most of the range was composed of rock crystals or quartz. The inhabitants of the small village of Cincora told him that, only thirty-five miles away, there was an ancient paved road set into the northern side of the mountain. It was a three-hour climb, they estimated, to reach the summit.

Further information came from a local cattle dealer, who related that he had once found a great cataract while penetrating some unexplored jungle. His description of the waterfall and of the surrounding terrain closely tallies with that of the manuscript. The dealer related how he had found, on the east bank of the waterfall, many deep mines and gaping tunnels in the mountainside. Traversing, these, he found that they led out to the edge of a plain, and it was here that he discovered a pit of extraordinary depth. Benigno must have listened with mounting excitement as the cattleman went on to tell him of a strange booming noise which was emitted from the mouth of the cavern, and which was caused, so he surmised, by a periodic inrush of water into some of the subterranean mine shafts. The noise, the dealer added, was like a cannon shot. He estimated that it would take Benigno about fifty days to reach the water-fall, a journey of about two hundred miles. Benigno also found out that there had long been a tradition in the area regarding an ancient city under a mountain, which had been overwhelmed by an earthquake and a flood, but before he was able to put this tantalizing information to use, he was stricken by the fever.

Twenty years or so after Benigno's ill-fated trip, the well-known traveller and author, Sir Richard Francis Burton, arrived in Rio to examine the *Relatório*. By this time (1865) it had been included among a set of papers known as the *Revista Trimensal*, published by the Instituto Histórico e Geographico Brasileiro. Commenting upon it in the second volume of his *Exploration of the Highlands of Brazil*, Sir Richard wrote that the tale of the deserted city was popularly supposed to be nothing more than a romance. He pointed out that the geographical clues in the account closely resemble the terrain surrounding a noisy waterfall on the São Francisco river known as the Great Rapids of Paulo Affonso. Burton also disclosed that near this fall, which was to be found about two hundred miles inland from the mouth of the river, there is a range of mountains called the Serra da Borracha, which in years gone by was called the Serra da Morebeca.

Another significant piece of information recorded by Sir Richard is the discovery of two strange hieroglyphs carved into the stone floor of a natural pothole or circular pit which he found a few miles from the São Francisco river. One of the glyphs is exactly similar to a character in the *Relatório*.

In the early 1900s, Colonel P. H. Fawcett, an ex-army surveyor, visited Rio and made a detailed study of the document. He took notes of the tribulations and of the conclusions reached by the unfortunate Benigno, passing on this information in the form of an almost blank map to a fellow adventurer, the former British Consul-General in Rio, Lieutenant-Colonel O'Sullivan. In 1913 O'Sullivan, accompanied by an Indian guide, set out from Bahia using Fawcett's information to plan his route to the lost city.

It seems that he did indeed stumble upon the ancient ruin, for he completed the map and gave it back to Fawcett, who duplicated the trip in 1921. In his memoirs Colonel Fawcett tells us that he went entirely alone, not fearing the Indians who were unlikely to attack a solitary traveller, and that the trip took three months to complete. He claimed to have found a ruined city, but was careful to leave no definite indication of where it was located. The few meagre clues that he did impart indicate that it was a very old walled city, entirely deserted and hidden in the jungle somewhere to the north of Bahia. One significant clue in his report is the description of a giant monolith of stone, crowned with a carved figure. A similar pillared statue is detailed within the pages of the *Relatório*. Of course, it must be pointed out that Fawcett was not looking for the Muribeca Mines, but for the lost city. His consuming passion was to discover the archaeological remains which, he was convinced, lay hidden in the impenetrable jungles of the Brazilian Highlands.

While most experts agree that the *Relatório* was genuinely written where and when it states, archaeologists strenuously deny the possibility of such a city being located in Brazil. However, it must be remembered that archaeology is not a very old science – about a hundred years at the most, whereas mining has been going on for many centuries. In recent years some rather astonishing facts have come to light that have caused archaeologists radically to change their views. In the case of Brazil it must be stressed that there is still a vast area of unexplored forest in which could be hidden a hundred cities like the one described in the manuscript – though it has been suggested that the *Relatório* is just an elaborate hoax, two hundred years old, and the possibility cannot be excluded. It is true that in the last few years the country has been increasingly networked by domestic airlines and no traces of ancient cities have been reported; on the other hand the airman Charles Lindbergh in the early 1930s saw a cyclopean stone wall deep in the jungle – a wall that stretched, he insisted, for many miles. Yet no explorer has ever been able to reach this wall overland. Geologists and naturalists who have worked in the area are of the opinion that the central plateau of Brazil is one of the world's most ancient land areas, having been above water at a time when most of the rest was submerged.

Colonel Fawcett placed the city further to the west than did Benigno. He maintained that on his three-month trip in 1921 the deserted city which he found was only twelve days' travel from Bahia and located in non-mountainous country, completely buried by the forest. It was not, he stated, the city mentioned in the manuscript of 1753 although it, too, had the remains of a statue on a great, black pedestal in the middle of a square. Fawcett was convinced that the city described in the *Relatório* would be found further inland on the high ground of Goiaz or Bahia Province.

The evidence does seem to suggest that Benigno was on the right track, and there is one further clue in the manuscript which may indicate the true site of the lost city. At the very beginning of the *Relatório*, on one of the sections that has been eaten away, can be deciphered the words 'Mestre de Can . . .' (Master of Can . . .). Two meanings can be attached to this. First, it may be a reference to the leader, or master, of the group of explorers. However, the phrase occurs at a point in the story where the writer is attempting to describe a location, and in the days when the manuscript was written it was common practice for the Portuguese to name ranges of hills Mestre de —— meaning master (ridge). The second possibility then is that the writer was referring to the Mestre de Canastra – the main ridge of the Serra do Canastra, located in the province of Minas Gerais. There is also a Canastra Range · in Goiaz Province.

Another area that has long been considered a likely site for the elusive city is the range of mountains known as the Serra do Roncador (Snorer's or Blusterer's Range). Not a great deal is known about these peaks, even today, but a modern map places them on the eastern edge of the Matto Grosso, four hundred miles north-east of Cuyaba – the town from which Fawcett set out on his last expedition from which he was never to return. At that time (1925) no one was certain of the precise position of the mysterious range. While making preparations for his trek into the unknown, Fawcett gleaned some of the local traditions from a rancher friend whose home was in the wild country, six days north of Cuyaba. The rancher told Fawcett that, ever since he was a boy, he and his people had sat on their verandah and listened to a strange noise which came periodically out of the northern forests. He described it as a hiss of a rocket or a great shell soaring into the air and plunging again into the forest with a 'boom-m-boom-m'.

On 14 April 1925 Fawcett wrote from Cuyaba of a conversation with an Indian tribesman from the remote northern interior. The Indian had described to one of the educated townspeople the existence of a great city near his tribal home. The city, the Indian said, had low stone buildings with many streets set at right angles to one another, but there were also some big buildings and a great temple in which was a large disc cut out of rock crystal. A river running through the forest beside the city fell over a big fall, whose roar could be heard for miles, and below the fall, in the quiet water of a lake, there was a figure of a man carved in white rock (probably crystal), which moved to and fro with the force of the current. Fawcett added that, although this sounded like the 1753 city, the location did not at all tally with his own calculations.

Fawcett's rancher friend had heard similar accounts from the few tribesmen of the north who wandered enough to make the journey into Cuyaba. The Indians, he told Fawcett, had many times spoken of the 'white mountain', probably meaning quartz crystal.

Although it is not impossible, it is highly unlikely that the Muribeca Mines and the adjacent city will be found in the Serra do Roncador, since the range is nearly a thousand air miles from the city of Bahia (which, incidentally, is now named San Salvador) and it seems unreasonable to suppose that the Muribeca himself penetrated so deeply into the continent to haul back his loads of silver ore. In 1967 an expedition included this mountain range in its programme, but no archaeological finds were reported – and during the last few years a road has been commissioned to drive right through to Cachimbo, which is in the remote north of Cuyaba. It may well pass close to the spot where Fawcett's Indians claimed their city lay. Only time will tell.

For those who are interested, there are two English translations of the *Relatório*. One was made by Lady Burton and published in an appendix to Sir Richard's book. The other has been published in Harold T. Wilkins' *Mysteries of Ancient South America*.

All the clues in the *Relatório* seem to suggest a location in the province of Bahia and it must be borne in mind that, even today, there is still a considerable amount of the central plateau that has not been explored by parties with the necessary interests. For instance, Benigno's cattle dealer had obviously discovered some sort of ancient mine workings, but thought little of his find, or at least made no attempt to capitalize on it. To the villagers of Cincora the existence of a dead city was merely a traditional tale; today its rediscovery would set the world of archaeology ablaze.

Petty Cache Accounts

Under the tongue-in-cheek title of this chapter I have put together four treasure stories which are less well documented than the others I have narrated but tell of hoards which, if found, would prove to be anything but petty.

The first of these is the strange tale of California's stranded pearl ship. Documents in the State Archives and the Naval Museum in Madrid, as well as others in Mexico City, tell the amazing story of a galleon that became marooned in the middle of the Californian desert. The tale begins in 1610 when Captain Alvarez de Cordone was summoned to appear before the Grand Viceroy in Mexico City. He was handed a commission from the King of Spain ordering him to fit out three ships and sail them into the Gulf of California on a pearl-hunting expedition. News of rich oyster beds in this area had filtered back to Mexico City and, true to form, the Spanish had made immediate plans to exploit them.

In the summer of 1612 the galleons were ready. With a crew of pearl divers aboard, they left Acapulco and sailed north up the coast towards the Gulf, gathering pearls from likely spots as they went. Before long the Spaniards encountered Indians and, in the ensuing fight, Cordone received an arrow wound serious enough to cause the flagship to put about and return to Acapulco. The other two vessels, under the commands of Captains Iturbe and Rosales, continued with the expedition, still moving slowly northwards until they reached the Gulf of California. It was here that Rosales' ship struck a submerged reef, irreparably damaging her hull. There was just time to transfer men, supplies, and of course the pearls, to Iturbe's vessel, before the stricken galleon sank.

For some reason Iturbe, with a now well-loaded ship, kept going rather than returning to the home port. He sailed up the Gulf until he reached a point where the River Colorado flows into it. Unknown to Iturbe, freak weather conditions had caused a severe flood over the area of southern California and Arizona, and the Colorado was swollen to such a size that it must have appeared part of the Gulf. Quite unwittingly, he sailed up this vast inland sea some two hundred miles from the actual mouth of the Colorado. Scientists of today have never been able to determine what caused this great flood, but it is certain that it took place. Iturbe may have thought that he had discovered a hitherto unknown passage between the Pacific and Atlantic oceans, something the Spaniards had been hoping to find for some time.

Iturbe continued north until the water became too shallow to proceed further and it was then that an alarming discovery was made. The water level was almost imperceptibly dropping. Hastily turning south, Iturbe made a run for it, only to find that the channel had dried up behind him. His galleon ran aground and the water evaporated until the ship was left virtually stranded in the middle of a desert. Taking all the supplies that they could carry, Iturbe and his crew set out on foot for Mexico City, abandoning the ship with her double cargo of pearls. The report made by the embarrassed Iturbe when he arrived went into the official maritime records in Mexico City.

In the years that followed probably only roving bands of Indians sighted the wreck; there remains a tradition of a 'great white bird in the desert', which may be based on the slowly disintegrating hulk with her tattered sails flapping in the hot desert air. The galleon remained 'lost' for over 160 years until 1775.

In October of that year Captain Juan Bautista de Anza of the Cavalry, Royal Presidio of Tubac, Sonora, Mexico (this ancient settlement is now located in southern Arizona) led 240 Spanish immigrants west across the desert towards the coast, where they later established a settlement that is today called San Francisco. As the party crossed the intervening desert, a scout is said to have discovered the remains of the ship and apparently investigated closely enough to find the rich cargo that she carried, because he deserted and struck across country to the south-west until he reached San Diego. Later he befriended some of the more peaceful Mohave Indians and recruited their help in searching for the galleon, but there is no record of him being successful.

In October 1863 an old prospector arrived at a desert encampment called Kane Springs, where he told how he had chanced upon the ship only a few days before. She was, he explained, now almost covered with shifting sand, and help would be required to dig out the treasure. An expedition was quickly organized which marched out of Kane Springs towards the south, but search as its members might, they could not relocate the missing galleon. In 1870 the New York *Galaxy* published the prospector's story and suggested that the galleon had been seen to the south of the road running to San Bernardino.

With the release of this article many more treasure hunters went into the desert to look for the buried galleon and in 1873 one expedition reported that they had found a ship's mast in the desert, '200 miles from the Gulf of California'.

The most significant historical detail relating to the ship, in the files of a California historical society, tells of a Norwegian settler, by name Nels Jacobsen, who owned a pig farm in an area to the south of the present-day Salton Sea, living there with his wife and a young ranch hand. The latter happened to mention in conversation with Jacobsen's wife that the teak of the heavy, odd-sized timbers out of which the pig pens were built was a strange wood to find in the desert. Mrs Jacobsen agreed and explained that the wood had come from an old ship that her husband had found in the desert. She made no effort to conceal this fact, and at the time, the ranch hand had not heard of the pearl galleon.

The young helper returned to the area, in later years and, going into the town of Brawley, asked about the Jacobsen family. He was surprised to hear that they had moved after selling their ranch for the staggering sum of 100000 dollars.

In 1905 the River Colorado flooded once more and water overflowed into the Imperial Valley, pouring into the Salton Sink, filling it to a depth of eighty-five feet. Thus the Salton Sea was born which now stretches thirty miles in length and fourteen miles across. This vast lake, some 235 feet below sea level, has been the source of a thriving business in salt extraction.

Although the tale of the lost pearl ship became widely known, the galleon still remained hidden and nothing more was heard of her until 1969, when a Californian resident reported seeing her from an aeroplane. According to his story, he and a companion were flying over the desert in 1967 when they saw the outlines of a ship that resembled an old pirate galleon. They had intended to try and find the place on the ground, but had not got around to doing so.

So far, the remains of the galleon have not been reported found, and if they are found it will be by sheer chance, when the winds of the desert blow the dunes away from the wreck. It sounds as if Nels Jacobsen got his hands on some of the treasure, but who knows, there may be a lot left.

Less strange but no less fascinating is the tale of the Dominican Republic's forgotten gold mine. Somewhere in the high cordillera of the Dominican Republic is said to lie a very deep mine of immense antiquity. The evidence regarding this lost mine is given in two books: one by George Hornius, the Dutch professor, in his *De Originibus Americis* (the 1652 edition); the other by Peter Martyr de Anghiera in the 1526 edition of his *De Orbe Novo*. Both books record the fact that Bartolomé Columbus – Christopher's brother – visited the mine in 1495.

Modern history begins for the Dominican Republic on 5 December 1492, when Christopher Columbus landed and established a garrison there. He christened the island Hispaniola (Little Spain), and it was said that he was forever ecstatic over its beauty, especially that of its mountains, which rise to over

10000 feet. In 1493 he sailed back to Spain leaving his brother Bartolomé as Governor of the garrison. The outpost flourished and became the first city: it was named Santo Domingo.

The native Arawaks, who called their island Hayti – 'the mountainous country' – greeted the Spaniards with the gift of gold, a sad error of judgement. Subsequent *conquistadores* exploited, enslaved and all but slaughtered them in their lustful search for the yellow metal.

Peter Martyr records that Bartolomé, acting on information given to him by the natives, made a trip into the high mountains with a troop of soldiers and miners and found the area from which the gold was mined. This, Peter tells us, lay some sixty leagues from the township of Isabella (Ysabella de Torres), on the north coast. When Bartolomé reached the spot, he saw that the pits extended over an area of about six miles, and he was extremely impressed by the obvious antiquity of the workings. The engineers on the expedition sank a few small shafts at several points and reported that there was enough gold in the soil for a miner to be able to extract 'six drachms a day', a considerable amount in those days.

George Hornius describes the mine as 'a cave, very high and very ancient, whence they say Solomon dug up his gold. This gold mine is 16000 feet deep and very ancient.' Bartolomé was certain that the mine was not dug by the natives. They had no traditional tales about them, were ignorant of the type of mining, and did not know who got their gold out of the rivers.

When judging the authenticity of the information given by these authors, we must note that Peter Martyr wrote only a scant thirty years after the actual date of Bartolomé's discovery, although the figure of 16000 feet given for the depth of the mine may seem exaggerated and is probably an error. George Hornius wrote about 167 years after the event and, although his information does tally with Martyr's, the figure of Spanish leagues (over 250 miles) is obviously misleading. The main range of mountains, called the Cordillera Central, stretches in a north-west/south-east direction across the island and, assuming that the lost mine is somewhere in this area, we find that it is a distance of about sixty *miles* (air miles, that is) to Isabella – or approximately *sixteen* Castilian leagues, a Castilian league being 4.2 miles. This probably explains the error.

Why then was this mine disregarded by the *conquistadores*? The answer may lie in the fact that, as the conquest of South America proceeded, the gold-hungry Spaniards discovered the unbelievable riches of Inca gold in Peru and the fabulous silver mines of Potosi. In the face of such overwhelming wealth, the significance of Bartolomé's mine declined rapidly, as did the importance of the garrison of Santo Domingo itself Another reason may be that the island's subsequent four hundred years of turbulent political history gave the residents more to think about than an old abandoned mine shaft.

Apart from the reference to the mine in the two books mentioned at the beginning of this story, there is evidence that the island was occupied in remote times by a race infinitely more cultured than the Arawaks found by Columbus. Strange caves were found by the early *conquistadores* of Hispaniola; one of these, named Jouanabaina, was on land owned by the Cacique of Machinech. It contained paintings on its walls and was worshipped by the natives. Similar caverns were found at Dubeda, among the Gonaives; in the Selle Mountains near Port-au-Prince; and at Doubou, near Cap François. Brasseur-de-Bourbourg, the famous nineteenth-century historian and *abbé* of the Mexican province of Chiappas, said in his writings that in the mountains of Haiti (and Santo Domingo) there existed great grottoes worked by man. According to the French traveller and naturalist, Michael-Etienne Descourtilz, the caverns were:

... natural excavations lit from the top, so as to let pass the first rays of the rising sun. The interiors of these grottoes are covered with idols, carved, engraved and inlaid in the rock, in rude, bizarre forms: toads with heads at the ends of their feet, monstrous human figures with crooked body diminishing like a cone, terminated by a spherical knob; tortoises: and other animals especially snakes.

Furthermore in his *Histoire des Caciques d'Haiti* the local author E. Nau tells us: 'There are vast crypts hollowed in the rock, walls of great extent and length in drystone, or only *en terre* [earthworks]. Another race, other men more polished in culture must have occupied this country in remote times.'

These grottoes of Haiti and the Dominican Republic sound very similar to the cave systems found recently in nearby Yucatan. They too are decorated with strange, carved figures and are of untold antiquity. Their discovery and the written evidence handed down from Bartolomé's expedition seem to provide a good case for the existence of the lost mine. The high part of the Cordillera Central, where the mine is most likely to be found, can be approached from two sides, since there are today good roads leading to the towns of José de las Matas on the northern slope of the mountains, and San Juan on the southern. Between these two towns are forty or fifty miles of heavily forested mountain, the highest point of which rises to 10200 feet.

From deep in the mythology of Indo-China comes the story of the vanishing wealth of Angkor Wat. Rumours still persist that large caches of treasure were hidden somewhere in the ruins of Angkor Wat and Angkor Thom, Cambodia's 700-year-old 'lost' city.

This archaeological wonder dates back to the end of the twelfth century when King Jayavarman VII (who reigned from 1181 to about 1215) ordered to be built in the centre of Angkor Thom a huge temple which he named Bayon. As the thirteenth century opened the King was gradually extending the Khmer empire to engulf practically the whole of Indo-China. His territory was exceedingly rich and one story which may typify the empire's affluence has persisted. It concerns the existence of a statue of Buddha, so encrusted with emeralds that it appears to be carved out of a single, gigantic stone. Whether this is fiction or fact, there is little doubt that Jaya-varman's wealth was considerable. After the King's death, however, the Khmer empire went into a slow decline.

Nevertheless, in the 1290s a commercial attaché of the Chinese Embassy, Chou Takuan (or Jou Da-gwan), paid a visit to Angkor Thom and found that it was still 'a prosperous land of gleaming gold-plated towers'. He wrote a diary of his experiences there, which describes in detail the wealth of the city and populace.

Above each gate there are five stone Buddhas, their faces turned towards the four cardinal points. The middle head is gilded. . . . A golden tower marks the centre of the kingdom. It is flanked by more than twenty stone towers and many hundreds of stone houses. A bridge of gold [he probably means that it was gilded] stretches from the east gate; two golden lions have been erected left and right of the bridge, and eight golden Buddhas stand below the stone galleries. . . . In the private apartments [of the Royal Residence] there is another golden tower. . . . The north gate has a square tower of gold, a lion and a Buddha in gold . . .

Later in the narrative, Chou describes part of the ceremony preceding an audience given by the King: 'After them walked the palace maidens. They passed by in their hundreds, carrying gold and silver vessels, trays of precious stones, ornaments, including ropes of pearls. . . .'

In 1431 the Siamese launched an all-out attack on Angkor Thom and the city was besieged for seven months. Eventually, some of the defenders, sympathetic to the invaders, betrayed the secrets of the underground entrances. Angkor Thom was captured and sacked but although the Siamese undoubtedly stripped the city of a great deal of its wealth, they did not find the real treasure, which was supposed to have been concealed in a walled crypt deep under the central sanctuary of the Bayon.

Of all the ruins in that area the Bayon is the most strange, built in such a manner as to give the impression of hoarding and overcrowding. In his recent book *Angkor and the Khmer Empire*, John Audric relates that 'There is always an uneasy feeling of being watched, even followed. It is inexplicable, but it exists and it is a sensation which many visitors share. . . . Wandering over its vast conglomeration of gloomy corridors . . . there is an irresistible impulse to glance furtively behind; and although no one is visible, one senses another presence.'

Since the rediscovery of Angkor Thom French archaeologists have reconstructed the larger part of the dilapidated city, mainly from the comprehensive descriptions found in Chou's account. The finds included a statue of the Buddha, dug up in 1933 from a pit beneath the central tower of the Bayon. But the legendary treasure has not been uncovered; it is, of course, said that the King took the most drastic measures to ensure that the secret of the cache was not revealed.

The last of my petty cache accounts is anything but small in size for it concerns the huge mysterious markers of the Cimarron.

In 1801, in the mountains of Colfax County, New Mexico, thirteen Frenchmen were panning for gold – a method of making a fortune that can be slow. The impatient Frenchmen soon found that a quicker way to wealth was to raid the other prospectors, and over a period of several months they killed twenty or so miners, losing six of their own men in the consequent fights. The remaining seven hired a Spanish resident of Santa Fe, by name José Lopat, to melt their store of gold dust and nuggets into five hundred ingots each weighing seven and a quarter pounds.

By 1804 these activities had aroused the fury of the other prospectors to such a degree that the Frenchmen were forced to move out of the area. They made careful plans to ship the gold overland to New Orleans, where they could embark for France. With Lopat as their guide the seven set out with six cart-loads of gold and headed for Oklahoma. In the late summer they made a halt at a watering hole known as Flag Springs and while they were encamped heard from local mountain men of the Louisiana Purchase. This extension of United States territory raised the knotty question of whether the US authorities would allow them to take the gold out of the country; after some discussion the Frenchmen decided that two of their number would ride ahead to New Orleans and discover the new regulations while the rest would stay at Flag Springs and guard the gold shipment. The Spaniard Lopat, no longer needed, returned to Santa Fe.

After waiting patiently for the first few months of 1805, the men at Flag Springs were forced to conclude that their two scouts were not going to return. They thought that the moment had now come when it was safer to cache the gold and return for it at a later date; so they buried it in the vicinity of the Springs.

Sometime later (the exact date is not known) one of the Frenchmen returned to Santa Fe. It is said his name was Father Pierre LaFarge, and he was an excommunicated priest who had served a prison sentence for killing a nun but still went under the guise of a padre. LaFarge met Lopat and told him that all his companions had been killed and that he, LaFarge, had returned to New Mexico to live in the higher altitude because he had contracted tuberculosis. In the time that he stayed in Santa Fe he grew gradually worse until he was bedridden.

Two of the sons of the miners that LaFarge and his friends had killed and robbed found out that the former priest was in Santa Fe and organized a lynching party but LaFarge escaped in a cart loaded with straw, according to Lopat, who added that LaFarge had died two weeks after his getaway.

Unfortunately LaFarge took the secret of the gold with him to his grave but he had mentioned more than once to Lopat that it 'was buried near the Spring'. Lopat assumed this to be Flag Springs and on this scant information set out to try and locate the cache. When he arrived at the waterhole, however, he had no idea where to dig and eventually gave up and returned home. In later years he told the whole story to his son, who wrote it down and stuck the pages in the back of the family Bible.

In 1878 three gigantic stone markers were discovered in the Sugar Loaf Peak area of Cimarron County, Oklahoma. Each of the markers is about a quarter of a mile in length and constructed of stone or rocks firmly embedded in the topsoil. They have been built to represent symbols, each one different. So far only one symbol has been readily identified, that of the Roman numeral XI, which forms the south-west corner marker. The other two markers were situated six miles to the north, and six miles to the east, thus forming an L shape.

It was not until the mid-1960s that the story of the Frenchmen's gold and the markers were linked, when a fourth marker was discovered precisely nine miles north of the south-east symbol. Again, the symbol it represents shows no similarity to those of the other three. A geologist who examined all four markers pronounced that they had been there for over a hundred years. When the positions of the markers were traced on to a map and lines centred across them, it was found that the geographical centre indicated a spot between Sugar Loaf Peak and the Cimarron River, near to Flag Springs. It was then concluded that the Frenchmen had constructed the markers in order to pinpoint the position of their buried cache.

The four symbols are so placed that they form an imperfect square, encompassing a vast area of more than forty square miles. To make a comparison: if you were to stand in Trafalgar Square each marker would stretch from Nelson's Column down to the Embankment at Charing Cross. And if Trafalgar Square is assumed to be the position of the south-west marker, the symbol immediately north would be at Wood Green, while the one to the east would be just beyond the Blackwall Tunnel. The remaining symbol would lie to the north-east, out almost as far as Waltham Abbey.

But why did the Frenchmen deem it necessary to work on such a large scale? The suggestion that the geographical centre is the 'X' which marks the cache seems too obvious, too convenient. Anyone who went to that amount of trouble to mark a cache is hardly likely to make it so easy to solve the problem. Obviously the symbols have been made as large as they are in order that they may be seen either from a distance or from a height – maybe from Sugar Loaf Peak?

The markers are located in the present-day Cy Strong Ranch, which covers 19000 acres north-west of Boise City. The treasure, estimated to be worth about £800000, still awaits discovery.

List of further reading

Audric, John Edward M., *Angkor and the Khmer Empire*. London: Hale, 1972.

Blavatsky, H. P., *Isis Unveiled*, 2nd ed., 2 vols. New York: J. W. Bruton, 1877.

Burton, Sir Richard Francis, *Exploration of the Highlands of Brazil*, 2 vols. London: Tinsley Bros., 1869.

Campbell, Sir Malcolm, *My Greatest Adventure : Searching for Pirate Treasure in Cocos Island*. London: Thornton Butterworth, 1869.

Charroux, Robert, *Treasures of the World*, trans. by Gloria Cantù. London: Frederick Muller, 1966.

Daniken, Erich von, *The Gold of the Gods*. London: Souvenir Press, 1973.

Davis, Britton, *The Truth About Geronimo*. London: Oxford University Press, 1929.

Fawcett, Lt-Col. P. H., *Exploration Fawcett*, arr. by Brian Fawcett. London: Hutchinson, 1953.

Furneaux, Rupert, *On Buried and Sunken Treasure*. Harmondsworth: Longman Young Books, 1973.

Prodgers, Cecil H., *Adventures in Bolivia*. London: John Lane, 1922.

Stephens, John Lloyd, *Incidents of Travel in Central America*. New York: Dover Publications, 1969.

Thomas, Athol, *Forgotten Eden*. London: Longman, 1973.

Wilkins, H. T., *Mysteries of Ancient South America*. London: Rider, 1946.